CHALLENGES IN MENTAL HEALTH AND POLICING

Key Themes in Policing series

Series editors: **Megan O'Neill**, University of Dundee, **Marisa Silvestri**, University of Kent and **Stephen Tong**, Kingston University

---

The Key Themes in Policing series is designed to fill a growing need for titles which reflect the importance of incorporating 'research informed policing' and engaging with evidence-based policing within Higher Education curricula.

Forthcoming in the series:

Practical Psychology for Policing
Jason Roach, January 2022

Out now in the series:

Towards Ethical Policing
Dominic Wood, April 2020

Critical Perspectives on Police Leadership
Claire Davis and **Marisa Silvestri**, March 2020

Police Occupational Culture
Tom Cockroft, March 2020

Policing the Police
Michael Rowe, February 2020

Miscarriages of Justice
Sam Poyser, Angus Nurse and **Rebecca Milne**, May 2018

Key Challenges in Criminal Investigation
Martin O'Neill, February 2018

Plural Policing
Colin Rogers, March 2016

Understanding Police Intelligence Work
Adrian James, April 2016

Find out more at

bristoluniversitypress.co.uk/key-themes-in-policing

CHALLENGES IN MENTAL HEALTH AND POLICING

Key Themes and Perspectives

Ian Cummins

First published in Great Britain in 2022 by

Policy Press, an imprint of
Bristol University Press
University of Bristol
1–9 Old Park Hill
Bristol
BS2 8BB
UK
t: +44 (0)117 374 6645
e: bup-info@bristol.ac.uk

Details of international sales and distribution partners are available at
policy.bristoluniversitypress.co.uk

British Library Cataloguing in Publication Data
A catalogue record for this book is available from the British Library

ISBN 978-1-4473-6083-4 hardcover
ISBN 978-1-4473-6084-1 paperback
ISBN 978-1-4473-6085-8 ePub
ISBN 978-1-4473-6086-5 ePdf

Cover design: Andrew Corbett
Front cover image: julietarts
Bristol University Press and Policy Press use environmentally responsible print partners.
Printed and bound in Great Britain by CMP, Poole

For Marilyn, Elliot, Nelson and Eilidh

Contents

List of figures and tables

Acknowledgements

As with all the other projects that I have undertaken, I am immensely grateful to my friends and family for the love and support that they have offered me over the years. I owe a huge debt to my late mother, who worked incredibly hard to ensure that I was able to take advantage of the educational opportunities that I was offered. She was also a lover of books; I hope that she would have enjoyed this one. My brother and sisters have been a constant source of support throughout my life. I am fortunate to have a great circle of friends and colleagues – a special thanks to Cliff and Lisa Bacon, Elaine Beaumont and Su Massey, Stuart Bowman, George Brown, the late and much missed Dr Allister Butler, Andy Davies and Selina Todd, John Devaney, David Edmondson, Marian Foley, Maria Grant, Victoria Gregson, Stephen Jones, Emma Kelly, Karen Kinghorn, Martin and Penny King, Jane Lucas, Lisa Morriss, Kate Parkinson and Stuart Case, David Platten, Nick Platten, Nicoletta and Dino Policek, Muzammil Quraishi, Jane Senior, Jonathan Simon, everyone in the Social Policy team at Salford and Louise Wattis.

I am grateful to everyone at Policy Press for their ongoing support of my work. I would like to thank the anonymous initial reviewers of this proposal for their detailed and constructive comments and suggestions. I have tried to incorporate them into the final version. Of course, any errors or omissions are my responsibility alone.

I am very grateful to Alice Park for the contributions to this volume.

Series preface

Megan O'Neill, Marisa Silvestri and Stephen Tong

The *Key Themes in Policing* Series aims to provide relevant and useful books to support the growing number of policing modules on both undergraduate and postgraduate programmes. The series also aims to support all those interested in policing from criminology, law and policing students, policing professionals to those who wish to join policing services. It seeks to respond to the call for research in relevant and under-researched areas in policing encouraged by organisations such as the College of Policing in England and Wales. By producing a range of high-quality, research-informed texts on important areas in policing, contributions to the series support and inform both professional and academic policing curriculums.

Representing the tenth publication in the series, *Challenges in Mental Health and Policing: Key Themes and Perspectives*, by Ian Cummins, explores the new landscape of policing and mental health considering historic factors that have led to the current position. Considering approaches from other countries and models of good practice that might be useful to the UK, this book focuses attention on England and Wales when considering legal issues, the broad policing role and acknowledges the intense public scrutiny directed on the police. This book acknowledges the limitations of the police, unable to be mental health nurses or social workers, but also emphasises the importance of providing safety to vulnerable individuals and appropriate follow-up care.

Ian Cummins is Senior Lecturer at Salford University. Before taking up a post as an academic, Ian worked as a probation officer and is a qualified social worker. Ian is widely published on mental health and the criminal justice system. He has conducted research and analysis in relation to social policy, social work, policing, community care and welfare. He has acted as a reviewer for *Routledge Criminology*, *British Journal of Social Work*, *Journal of Social Work Education*, *International Journal of Social Work*, *Journal of Forensic Psychiatry and Psychology*, *Journal of Academy of Social Science* and *Journal of Adult Protection and Transgressive Culture*. He is also a reviewer of research bids for the National Institute for Health Research Central Commissioning Facility and is a member of the editorial board of the *Journal of Adult Protection*.

Introduction

The use of language is a difficult area in the mental health field. Language is vitally important in conveying meaning but also status and symbolic value. It can also be used in discriminatory, insulting and stigmatising ways. This is clearly the case in the area of mental health. The issues here are complex and messy – usage changes quickly and so on. In this volume, the terms people with mental health issues or problems are mainly used. I accept that some might object to this usage. No offence is intended. One of the dilemmas here is that any term has the potential to imply that there is a distinct group of people or that they are somehow separate from the rest of the population. This is the opposite of my value and ideological positions. Mental health and illness are central features of the human condition.

We should never lose sight of the fact that people with mental health problems come into contact with the police in the same ways as any other citizens – as witnesses, victims of crimes and as work colleagues. The volume outlines the key themes and debates in the world of policing and mental health. It seeks to explore the drivers of this shift in focus as well as challenging some of the established notions in the field. The nature of the police role in mental health work is becoming more complex. The long-standing failings to meet the progressive vision of well-resourced community mental health services (Cummins, 2020d) mean that police contacts with people with mental health problems have increased. The focus on partnership and other forms of interdisciplinary working has also meant a greater police mental health role. In this field, the focus is usually on the police response to emergencies. This can distort the view of police mental health work. Increased demands in this area have led to an organisational push-back from the police, concerned that they are taking on the work of other organisations. On an individual level, officers feel frustrated and lacking in confidence about how to respond to mental health emergencies. These issues form the policy and organisational backdrop to this volume.

The workings of the criminal justice system (CJS) are paradoxically hidden and exposed. Most of us have little real contact with the main institutions of the CJS – police, courts and prisons. However, the majority probably hold quite strong views about how those institutions should function and on wider penal policy. The length of sentences, the conditions in prisons and high profile cases all generate significant media coverage and debate. This should be the case in an open society. Pre-COVID-19, crime and crime drama dominated the news and TV schedules. High profile crimes dominate the news media but also lead to broader debates about the nature of society. The Overton window on debates about law and order has shifted significantly towards the political right in the past 40 years (Cummins, 2021). However, at the same time, as an institution, the police have come under increasing scrutiny and criticism from both the right and the left. The extent of postwar deference and respect for the police has been exaggerated by a nostalgic desire for a return to community values. In this nostalgic construction, the British police officer was an avuncular Dixon of Dock Green figure embedded in the community and widely respected. Modern critical scrutiny of the police occurs at an individual, organisational and operational level. This is the case from commentators across the political spectrum. Those on the right see the modern police force as being too concerned with issues such as diversity and inclusion. The view here is that the police cannot protect the public because they focus on allegedly side issues such as online hate speech at the expense of real crime. On the left, these organisational commitments to diversity and inclusion are seen as masking the fact that the police organisational culture remains at its core racist, misogynist and homophobic, dedicated to serving the interests of capital and defending the class interests of elites.

Police mental health work

Societal attitudes to mental health have changed significantly over the past 50 years. The pace of that change has been even faster since the election of the Coalition government in 2010. A more open and honest approach, including celebrity led campaigns, means that people are more willing to discuss mental health experiences. Increased awareness brings increased recognition. One further possible outcome of this is that people are more likely to disclose a mental health issue during an encounter with the police. Another is that there is much wider recognition of the potential psychological impact of being a police officer. This is a hugely important and welcome move. There is much work still to be done, but this volume discusses organisational policies to support officers in maintaining good mental health that would have virtually unimaginable ten years ago. The new Police Education Qualifications Framework (PEQF), which seeks to professionalise police education and training, can also play a key role here.

One of the most striking features of the police and mental health landscape is how the same issues arise across many countries. An increase in police encounters because of the historic failings of the policy of deinstitutionalisation, exacerbated by recent policies of public service retrenchment and leading to increased police frustration. It is important to underline here that these factors lead to poor outcomes for the most vulnerable and marginalised citizens.

These poor outcomes include stigmatising and potentially criminalising interventions, delayed access to appropriate mental health care, the excessive use of force and even fatalities. People with mental health issues are at much greater risk of being tasered or subject to other forms of force. Police officers have long raised concerns that they are not properly trained to respond to mental health emergencies. This uncertainty could lead to the misunderstanding of actions by distressed individuals. Frontline officers struggle to adapt their approach to a mental health crisis. Lack of police training and confidence in dealing with such situations is a factor here. The person in crisis may not understand the police involvement or respond to police directions, which further increases the likelihood that force will be used. These risks are increased in countries where frontline officers are routinely armed. In addition, it is important to consider issues of race as people from minority communities are at greater risk. A number of innovative police and interagency responses, such as the Crisis Intervention model in Memphis and Car 87 in Vancouver, have followed a fatal encounter between the police and an individual in mental health crisis. Finally, police interventions in these circumstances raise questions of police legitimacy, transparency and accountability. The police role cannot be viewed in isolation from the work of other mental health agencies. It is too reductionist to say that the involvement of the police indicates that other agencies have failed.

In exploring the new landscape of policing and mental health, this volume looks at the historical factors that have led to the current position. It also examines the lessons that we can learn from other countries and models of good practice that might be applicable to the UK. The focus of this volume, specifically when discussing legal issues, is England and Wales. There is different legislation that applies in Scotland and Northern Ireland but the range of police powers is similar. The police role has always been wider than the apprehension of offenders. In this wider public welfare role, officers have always been called upon to respond to citizens in crisis or situations that may be linked to a mental health issue, such as a person with dementia who goes missing. The police, like all public bodies, have been subject to greater public scrutiny. This has been part of the audit culture that is such a defining feature of the modern public sector. Changes in policy are often driven by responses to tragedies and failures. There have been a series of inquiries, inspection reports and House of Commons committee reports that have specifically examined policing and mental health alongside the wider experiences of people with mental health problems in the CJS. In addition, since the early 1990s there have been a series of inquiries into homicides by people with mental health problems that included a discussion of the police role.

Bittner (1990) suggested that the unique competence of the police was the ability to intervene in public and private situations. This was an attempt to capture the core police role as it extends across a huge variety of settings.

It is particularly relevant in the area of mental health. Police powers under section 136 of the current Mental Health Act (MHA) mean that they are the only professionals that have legal powers to intervene in emergency mental health crisis that in community settings. It is a well-documented frustration of frontline officers that they feel that they act as a sticking plaster. There is a lack of effective outcomes. This should not be dismissed as simply part of the policing professional outlook. It exposes the fault lines in mental health services. It is also the case that police interventions may, unintentionally, perpetuate rather than address the underlying factors that have created the crisis. This volume acknowledges the difficulties in this area. However, it is important while doing this to recognise that there are examples of innovative practice and models of working that are being developed to tackle long-standing issues. It is also important to acknowledge the work of individual officers. Frontline officers cannot be mental health nurses or social workers – society cannot expect them to be. The recent calls to 'defund the police' can be viewed as an argument for greater investment in health and welfare services. It is this investment that holds the key. In crisis situations, frontline officers should ensure that individuals are safe, and that family members and members of the public are safe. Following on from that, the aim is to ensure that a person in crisis receives appropriate mental health care, in a health setting, as soon as possible. On the surface this seems a straightforward aim. However, the pressures on mental health services mean that we are far from achieving this policy goal. The police cannot solve these issues in isolation. At the same time, this does not mean that there cannot be different approaches from the police that will assist in achieving this goal. Without wider investment in other areas then the likelihood is that the police will continue to be left 'picking up the pieces'.

Further reading

Her Majesty's Inspectorate of Constabulary and Fire and Rescue Services (2018) *Policing and mental health: picking up the pieces*. Available at: https://www.justiceinspectorates.gov.uk/hmicfrs/wp-content/uploads/policing-and-mental-health-picking-up-the-pieces.pdf

Home Affairs Select Committee (2018) *Policing for the future*. Available at: https://www.parliament.uk/business/committees/committees-a-z/commons-select/home-affairs-committee/inquiries/parliament-2017/policing-for-the-future-inquiry-17-19/

Teplin, L.A. (1984) Criminalizing mental disorder: the comparative arrest rate of the mentally ill. *American Psychologist*, 39(7), 794.

Thomas, S. (2020) Critical essay: fatal encounters involving people experiencing mental illness. *Salus Journal*, 8(2), 100.

Thomas, S. and Watson, A. (2017) A focus for mental health training for police. *Journal of Criminological Research, Policy and Practice*, 3(2), 93–104.

Wood, J.D., Watson, A.C. and Fulambarker, A.J. (2017) The 'gray zone' of police work during mental health encounters: findings from an observational study in Chicago. *Police Quarterly*, 20(1), 81–105.

1

Policing and society

Introduction

This chapter will explore some of fundamental questions about the nature of policing in a liberal democratic society. This chapter places mental health work in the wider context of the welfare role that police officers undertake. The chapter begins with a brief discussion of the broader politics of law and order of the past 40 years. There are two key claims made here. First, that the politics of law and order has shifted to the right. Second, the political success of the Thatcher and Reagan administrations meant that their political opponents tacked rightwards for the fear of being 'soft' on crime. Alongside this, neoliberal influenced policies saw the introduction of market mechanisms or practices into the public sector including the police. As in other areas of the public sector, policing was subjected to new forms of managerialism and audit. In addition, wider public confidence in the police was undermined. The police found themselves under pressure from both the left and the right. This crisis in police legitimacy is examined in this chapter, including calls for a new form of policing/public contract based on fundamental democratic values.

Thatcherism and the politics of law and order

The election of Margaret Thatcher in 1979 marked a huge shift in British politics. Thatcher's influence continues to be felt over 30 years since she left Downing Street. Hall (1979) coined the term 'Thatcherism' to describe the blend of traditional Conservative values and economic liberalism that her politics represented. It is also important not to overlook the confrontational approach to politics that was at the heart of Thatcherism. Thatcher developed and exploited a narrative that the nation was in crisis. She embodied the radical action that was required to solve these problems (Young, 2002). She rejected the social democracy of the post-1945 period, which she saw as being the root of the decline of Britain and a major factor in the crisis in the winter of 1978 that led to her General Election success. To her supporters, she became the 'Iron Lady', who had not only saved Britain from the chaos of the 1970s, but presided over an economic miracle and restored the country's standing in the world. Thatcher presented the state as being dominated by a liberal elite supported by progressives who opposed traditional values but who also despised 'ordinary people' (Hall, 1979). Penal policy provided an excellent example of this approach. A key recurring theme during and since that period is that the CJS has gone 'soft'. Thatcherism presented the CJS as being dominated by a liberal elite – elites are always presented as liberal (Hall, 1979). This elite, made up of civil servants, academics, penal reformers, *The Guardian* and other progressives, is too concerned with the rights of offenders, ties the hands of the police in the fight against crime, and marginalises victims. Penal populism involves politicians making direct calls to the electorate over the heads of these policy makers and influencers (Garland, 2004). It is part of a wider call to traditional social and community values. Penal populism sees the police fight against crime as being hampered by liberal concerns about rights and due process. Alongside this, it includes calls for longer prison sentences and harsher conditions in prisons with restrictions on prisoners' access to privileges (Cummins, 2021).

The rise in the use of imprisonment has been one of the most significant social and public policy developments of the past 40 years. It is most apparent in the US. There are now over two million people in US jails. A frequently quoted statistic is that the US has 5 per cent of the world's population, and over 25 per cent of the world's prisoners. In Europe, England and Wales have followed this trend most closely. The political success of Reagan and Thatcher meant that there was a rightwards shift in debates about law and order. Parties, nominally of the left or centre-left, moved to the right on these issues. In the UK, no politician has really sought to shift the debate back to the centre ground (Cummins, 2021). New Labour are the best example of this. Tony Blair's famous slogan 'Tough on crime, tough on the causes of crime' was a statement of intent and a determination not to be seen as weak or 'on the side of the offender'. From the 1990s onwards, after Thatcher had left office, penal policy did not become more centrist. In fact, penal policy was more Thatcherite after she left office (Cummins, 2021). Home Secretaries from both political parties took the view that 'prison works'. For example, the prison population in England and Wales increased by 41,800 to over 86,000 between June 1993 and June 2012. In his early days as Prime Minister, Boris Johnson, alongside his Home Secretary Priti Patel, made a series of policy announcements such as increasing the number of police officers and restricting the early release of offenders convicted of violent and sexual offences. These moves were strong echoes of the 'get tough' law-and-order Tory party policies of the late 1970s and early 1980s.

Simon (2007) argues that this period of the 'punitive turn' led to a new politics of law and order. He termed this process 'Governing through Crime'. This is fundamentally different to the process of managing criminal behaviour that all states undertake. In his work, Simon (2007) outlines the ways in which the perceived danger of being a victim of crime has had an impact on a range of behaviour and choices that citizens make. For example, the increase in sales of Sports Utility Vehicles (SUVs) in the US and the rise of the gated community. The politicalisation of the law and order question was a feature of the elections that returned neoliberal governments in the US and UK throughout the 1980s. Simon (2007) argues that the victim of crime, particularly violent crime, came to act as the dominant modality of citizenship. He provides several examples where violent crime has had a direct impact on the election process. The most famous of these is the case of Willie Horton, a convicted murderer, who raped a woman while he was on a period of weekend leave. This case was used by George Bush (Snr) in an attack advert on Dukakis in the 1988 presidential campaign. In the presidential campaigns of both 2016 and 2020, Trump used very similar approaches. In this case, he conflated immigration, crime and Black Lives Matters protests against police violence and brutality to play on middle-class anxieties about law and order. Schrag (2004) outlines the 'neo-populist' terms in which law and order debate are consistently framed. As already noted, this includes a strong suspicion and distrust of experts, policy makers and political elites (Garland, 2004). The political right has successfully exploited these populist themes. Simon (2007) observes that all violent crime poses difficult questions for governments whatever their political make-up. These problems are particularly acute for parties on the left as they were committed to the possibility of rehabilitation. The result has been an increase in the prison population fuelled by longer sentences and policies such as the 'three strikes' law in the US and the Imprisonment for Public Protection (IPP) sentences in England (Cummins, 2021).

New Labour and Left Realism

Hall (1979), in his analysis of Thatcherism, recognised that part of its appeal was the way that it exploited the law and order issue. This included unequivocal support for the thin blue line. This was not just some abstract philosophical position. It included a commitment to increase police pay as well as recruiting more officers. In addition, in a series of controversies in the 1970s and 1980s (miscarriages of justice cases such as the Birmingham Six; the riots of the early 1980s; the miners' strike; and Hillsborough), the Thatcher government provided the police with unquestioning public support. Thatcherism was also critical of progressive parties portraying criticism of the police and police tactics as being 'anti-police'. This was partly achieved by highlighting the weaknesses in the radical analysis of the role of the police and other agencies. Radical perspectives on policing see it as a form of class oppression, serving the interests of capital and help to sustain and perpetuate inequality and injustice. In this analysis, this has always been the ultimate role of the police. It not always necessarily apparent but it becomes most clear at times of crisis. The miners' strike of 1984–1985 is a clear example of this. The bitter dispute was a brutal clash between the National Union of Miners (NUM) committed to defending jobs and the Thatcher government, which was committed to destroying 'militant' trade unionism. Thatcher herself had been a member of the Heath government in the 1970s that had been defeated on two occasions in disputes with the NUM. She was determined that she would not lose a third time. The miners were labelled by Thatcher as 'The Enemy Within'. Throughout, it was very clear that the role of the police was to ensure that non-striking miners could continue to work and that stocks of coal were moved to power stations. In the most politicised industrial dispute since the General Strike, which divided the country, it was clear whose interests policing was serving (Reiner, 1985; Green, 1990; Buckley, 2015).

From a radical perspective, any reforms or commitment to diversity cannot mask the fundamental role of the police and the class interests that they serve (Vitale, 2017; Purnell, 2021). The role of the police cannot be divorced from wider neoliberal policies and the attack on the welfare state (Garrett, 2017). For example, as well as attacking trade unionists, Thatcher and her supporters in the tabloid press also demonised already marginalised groups including the poor, welfare claimants, immigrants and offenders (Cummins, 2021). These processes were racialised, as the analysis in *Policing the crisis* (Hall et al, 2013) showed.

The debates about law and order in the late 1970s and early 1980s continue to resonate. They crystallise debates about the role of the police. The radical focus on the police role as a tool of capitalist oppression failed to analyse fully the other functions of the police. More critically, it failed to take account of the fact that the most vulnerable and marginalised communities were the ones that need police protection most. These communities were overpoliced and underprotected – for many commentators this is still the case. The Left Realism school of criminology – mostly closely associated with Jock Young – argued that progressive politics had to engage with the realities and impact of crime. In particular, it argued that it was important not to surrender the political ground to Thatcherite views. It was only by acknowledging the impact of crime that support for different models of penal policy could be developed. The most important factor here is that working-class people are more likely to be victims of crime and that the impact of crime is most keenly felt in working-class neighbourhoods.

Left Realism

Left Realism sought to combine the radical critiques of the crimes of elites, state and corporations with this recognition that crime inflicts harm and pain on individuals and communities (Matthews, 2010). Left Realism argued that the critical criminology as represented by Hall et al (2013) had been naïve in seeing criminals as class warriors challenging the capitalist system (Lea, 1987, 1992, 2002). Lea (2016) argued that Left Realism developed as a reaction to the poles of Conservative law-and-order policies and what he terms 'Left Idealism'. This is the term he uses for the work of Hall et al (2013) and others such as Gilroy (1982, 2013) that failed to engage with the reality of crime. Both perspectives lead to a situation where working-class communities experienced the worst of both worlds: high crime and ineffective, often racist police practices such as the disproportionate use of stop and search powers. Lea (1987, 1992) outlined what he termed the 'square of crime', with the four corners being victims, offenders, the public and state agencies. The aim of Left Realism was to improve the relations between these four groups. One potentially fruitful approach to the analysis of Left Realism is to regard it as a reaction to the popular and electoral successes of Thatcherism. Matthews (2010) argues that Left Realism sought to produce an account and response to crime that recognised the genuine harms that individual criminal acts could inflict on victims while, at the same time, not diminishing the harms caused by the crimes of the state and corporations.

Thatcherite rhetoric focused on the impact of crime on victims. This was a powerful and popular message that excluded any account of the crimes of the elite or broader notions of social harm. Crime is simply a matter of individual morality and any attempts to examine broader social issues such as poverty, racism and inequality are viewed as ways of allowing offenders to escape individual responsibility for their own actions (Hall and Wilson, 2014). The logic of this approach also leads to calls for more resources and powers for the police to assist them in their fight against crime. Alongside this, there is a view that the CJS and the law works in favour of offenders rather than the law-abiding majority. In populist discourse, the police are fighting the war against crime with their hands tied behind their backs by the liberal elite. This model requires that there is a strong commitment to support the police. Any critical views are seen as an attempt to undermine the police as an institution and weaken their effectiveness. Once the police have brought offenders to justice, there is a need for strong and effective punishments. As Michael Howard, Home Secretary, famously said in 1993, 'prison works'. By this he meant it not only punishes the guilty but it acts as a deterrent to others. Prison also plays the symbolic role in recognising the societal harm offending causes.

Lea (1987, 1992, 2002) argued that critical criminology held naïve and Romantic views of offenders as rebels and class warriors. These views ignored the fact that crime had a disproportionate impact on working-class communities. It allowed the populist ideas to dominate. There are wider political implications here. For example, Thatcher's tough stance on law and order was a key part of her political image but was also undoubtedly popular with a significant proportion of the electorate. By failing to provide a realistic alternative, progressives were surrendering political territory and capital. Left Realism was most influential in the early years of New Labour. Blair's 'Tough on crime, tough on the causes of crime' is one possible neat summary of Left Realism. However, Young and others became disillusioned with what they saw as the more punitive approaches adopted (Cummins, 2021). Even though she left office over 30 years ago, Margaret Thatcher casts a long shadow over British politics. Nowhere is that more apparent than in penal policy.

Policing, democracy and legitimacy

What is the role of the police? At face value, the answer to this question seems straightforward. The role of the police is surely to prevent crime and apprehend offenders. However, this definition ignores the broader welfare role that policing entails as well the complex organisational structures and partnership working that are common across the modern public sector. Policing is deeply embedded in these structures. As already noted, other public and private agencies are increasingly taking on policing roles and tasks. Aspects of police work are being outsourced. This volume is concerned with the police role in mental health work and more broadly work that protects or ensures the safety of vulnerable people. Any definition of policing that does not acknowledge this is at best a partial and at worst a misleading one. In examining the wider police role, this section will begin with a consideration of the work of sociologists such as Bittner (1970) who developed the academic study of policing and police organisational culture. This work highlighted that police officers are involved in a whole range of work that is not specifically concerned with crime. It also demonstrated that the police exercise significant discretion in the application of their legal powers, with arrest often being a last rather than a first resort.

The 1960s saw the beginning of a body of ethnographic research into modern policing. This was part of the development of critical perspectives in criminology that examined the role of the police and the wider CJS. Becker's (2008) work on labelling and deviance was hugely influential here. The police and other professionals such as social workers and psychiatrists play key roles in the construction and management of 'deviant' individuals and communities. The nostalgia view of the police as the neutral upholders came under critical scrutiny, as did the police organisational culture. From this point onwards, the notion of police culture became a key theoretical lens for the analysis of policing (Cockcroft, 2014). This critical perspective challenged the notion of the police as a formal command and control organisation where rules were followed in a bureaucratic fashion. This bureaucracy was supported by a military style rank hierarchy with a strict code of discipline. This image, in part a result of the Peelian principles discussed in the next section, was also an attempt to present the police as impartial enforcers of the rule of law (Reiner, 2010).

Peelian principles reconsidered

Grieve (2015) notes that there is no evidence that Sir Robert Peel actually wrote the principles that bear his name. However, they have taken on mythic status as the bedrock of the notion of British 'policing by consent' (Loader, 2016).

Peelian principles

- To prevent crime and disorder, as an alternative to their repression by military force and severity of legal punishment.
- To recognize always that the power of the police to fulfil their functions and duties is dependent on public approval of their existence, actions and behaviour, and on their ability to secure and maintain public respect.
- To recognize always that to secure and maintain the respect and approval of the public means also the securing of the willing cooperation of the public in the task of securing observance of the law.
- To recognize always that the extent to which the cooperation of the public can be secured diminishes, proportionately, the necessity of the use of physical force and compulsion for achieving police objectives.
- To seek and preserve public favour, not by pandering to public opinion, but by constantly demonstrating absolutely impartial service to law, in complete independence of policy, and without regard to the justice or injustice of the substance of individual laws, by ready offering of individual service and friendship to all members of the public, without regard to their wealth or social standing, by ready exercise of courtesy and good humour, and by ready offering of individual sacrifice in protecting and preserving life.
- To use physical force only when the exercise of persuasion, advice and warning is found to be insufficient to obtain public cooperation to an extent necessary to secure observance of law or restore order; and to use only the minimum degree of physical force which is necessary on any particular occasion for achieving a police objective.
- To maintain at all times a relationship with the public that gives reality to the historic tradition that the police are the public and that the public are the police; the police being only members of the public who are paid to give full-time attention to duties which are incumbent on every citizen in the interests of community welfare and existence.

- To recognize always the need for strict adherence to police-executive functions, and to refrain from even seeming to usurp the power of the judiciary of avenging individuals or the state, and authoritatively judging guilt and punishing the guilty.
- To recognize always that the test of police efficiency is the absence of crime and disorder and not the visible evidence of police action in dealing with them. (Loader, 2016, pp 429–30)

In his analysis of Peelian principles, Loader (2016) acknowledges that on the surface there is little to object to in them. They appear to have served as the ethical basis for policing for nearly 200 years. There is little within them that one could fundamentally object to. However, the 'motherhood and apple pie' nature of Peelian principles creates a series of difficulties.

Policing is a complex, messy and times contradictory business. In such a setting, some discursive principles have an advantage over a set of legal rules that would struggle to cover all situations. Loader (2016) argues Peelian principles are so vague that they become meaningless in the context of modern policing. They cease to become guides for the role but become statements about the nature of the role. For example, Loader (2016) notes that principle two, 'The power of the police to fulfil their functions and duties is dependent upon public approval', is simply a statement about policing in a democratic society. It does not give any indication or guidance about how that public approval is sought or what should happen if it is removed.

Peelian principles need to be placed in their historical context – assuming that they were actually developed in the 1820s. They are part of the development of the institutions of the modern state. In many ways, their longevity can be viewed as a form of nostalgia for a golden age of community and the police role in maintaining order. Loader (2016) argues that they are not sufficiently robust to meet the challenges of contemporary policing and police governance. The principles assume police legitimacy rather than providing answers to fundamental questions such as how to generate and maintain it. Police legitimacy has been brought into wider question by a series of events such as the miscarriages of justice in the 1970s, the police role in the 1984/1985 miners' strike, Hillsborough and the undercover cop scandals. The public has become more critical of institutions generally, including the police (Loader and Mulcahy, 2003). In addition, the fact that the police are working in more unequal societies (Millie and Bullock, 2013) means that it becomes even more difficult to demonstrate the 'absolute impartiality' that Peelian principles claim as a fundamental bedrock of policing. From a radical perspective, the Peelian principles are a form of sophistry that is used to mask the real purpose of policing, which is the defence of class interests. There is also a form of British exceptionalism at work here. British policing is being presented as 'policing by consent' and as fundamentally different to other models of policing. Loader (2016) concludes that Peelian principles have become mythologised. Like all myths they are powerful. They provide a comforting notion that British policing has always been by consent and this sets it apart from other models and practices (Brogden and Nijhar, 2005).

Loader (2016) seeks to recast Peelian principles for modern democratic societies taking account of modern human rights perspectives. He notes that Peelian principles appear designed to govern contacts between the police and the public. They provide little in the way of guidance for the broader context of police work and the modern inspection and audit framework. They have no legal status. Despite this, they continue to act as a point of reference for wider societal notions of policing. They also provide a stronger narrative structure for how the police sees itself as an institution. This is despite the fact that policing the modern digital, globalised and interconnected environment (Weisburd and Neyroud, 2011; Aas, 2014) is a world away from the London of the 1830s. One of the most significant features of the modern policing landscape is that there an increasing number of public and private bodies that take on regulatory and policing functions. The Peelian principles were developed in an environment that did not need to consider this issue. The result is a gap. The public and private agencies will have mission statements and codes of conduct that include echoes of Peel. However, the relationship between the police, agencies and the public is more complex. Loader concludes that the major weakness of Peelian principles is that they have no legal standing. A final limitation flows from the status of these principles, both legal and socio-cultural. The problem in the former instance can be easily stated: Peelian principles have no institutional standing or legal force. Any failure to follow them does, therefore, have little or no impact within the regulation, inspection and audit framework.

Loader's modern Peelian principles

Loader (2016) proposes the following as principles that can underpin policing in modern democratic societies:

- The basic mission of the police is to improve public safety and wellbeing by promoting measures to prevent crime, harm and disorder.
- The police must undertake their basic mission with the approval of, and in collaboration with, the public and other agencies.
- The police must seek to carry out their tasks in ways that contribute to social cohesion and solidarity.

- The police must treat all those with whom they come into contact with fairness and respect.
- The police must be answerable to law and democratically responsive to the people they serve.
- The police must be organized to achieve the optimal balance between effectiveness, cost-efficiency, accountability and responsiveness.
- All police work should be informed by the best available evidence.
- Policing is undertaken by multiple providers, but it should remain a public good.

These principles recognise the realities and complexities of modern policing. Loader's new principles can act as the basis for the democratic oversight of policing – on both an individual and organisational level. They recognise that policing is carried out by myriad agencies. In addition, the principles embed wider ones of citizenship and the modern human rights framework within them. The police must not only serve communities but be as representative of them as possible.

Conclusion

Classic ethnographic research in policing highlighted the extent of police discretion (Bittner, 1970) but also the range of tasks that policing involves (Punch, 1979). The cultural representation of the police has focused one aspect of the role – apprehending offenders. Even then, this focus narrows to one aspect of that role, the arrest of high profile and violent offenders (Cummins et al, 2014). Reiner's (1992a) classic and hugely influential study outlined elements of a police organisational culture that was the result of a focus on 'thief taking'. The culture he outlined was action focused with an essentially cynical and pessimistic view of the world and the communities that police officers were meant to be protecting. The culture was a hyper-masculine one in which misogyny, homophobia and overt racism was tolerated and not challenged. The 'thin blue line' was required to prevent society collapsing into anarchy. This created a strong police family identity which was a source of protection for individual officers. It also meant that wrongdoing, the misuse of force, racism and corruption were much less likely to be exposed.

There is a danger in failing to recognise that all cultures are dynamic and individuals make their way through them. There have been huge changes in policing and the wider society since Reiner (1992a) analysed cop culture. These include very different social and organisational attitudes in the areas of race, gender and sexuality. In acknowledging progress, it is important to recognise the impact of discriminatory attitudes on individuals and wider police community relations. Change comes about by organisations recognising the need to change but also recruiting from more diverse backgrounds. A series of reports including Scarman (1981) and the Macpherson Inquiry (1999) had, for example, outlined the institutionalised racism of policing. The Gay Police Association was formed in 1990 with the aim of promoting equal opportunities for gay and bisexual men and women in the police, offering advice and support, and improving relations between the police service and the wider gay community. The 1970s world of policing was satirised by the TV dramas *Life on Mars* and *Ashes to Ashes*. The figure of DI Gene Hunt embodied macho, racist, homophobic and misogynist police culture – he was also violent towards suspects. The series were both huge successes. Hunt became something of a cultural icon – for traditionalist he was not a figure to satirise but represented a Britain and an approach to policing that had been lost. The demise of Gene Hunts symbolised for commentators such as Peter Hitchens how modern policing had been emasculated by criminal justice reform and diversity policies.

There have clearly been huge cultural and organisational shifts since the 1970s. As an institution the police is governed like others, and has to ensure that it complies with a range of legislation and policies that seek to ensure equality of treatment and opportunity for all individuals. This includes in the areas of recruitment and employment as well as the service that is provided to the wider community. However, organisational change requires more than the introduction of policy documents. It requires an ongoing commitment to tackling issues and challenging unacceptable behaviour or attitudes. More recent research has shown that despite this organisational commitment to change some of the features of police culture that Reiner outlined remain strong (Loftus, 2010). Policing reflects the wider society. Some of these issues can only be tackled on a fundamental and societal level. The police can and must be part of these processes but they cannot achieve them on their own. Neoliberal social, economic and welfare policies have exacerbated the inequalities that are at the root of these issues. Policing forms part of the social contract agreed between society and citizens. It operates within a distinct political and social context – it influences that context but clearly it is only one of the factors at play.

The notion that the sole function of the police is to prevent crime and bring offenders to justice has never really withstood much detailed scrutiny. The COVID-19 pandemic has highlighted among many other things the way that unforeseen events lead to new roles for and demands on police resources. Alongside these challenges the nature of crime and criminal investigation changes. For example, the use of social media, closed-circuit television (CCTV) and mobile phone use means that the police have new technologies available in investigation. It also means that huge amounts of data are created that could hold the key to investigation. The analysis of CCTV and mobile phone records can be hugely labour-intensive and time-consuming. New technology also creates the opportunity for new forms of criminal activity such as online fraud. In addition, communities are becoming more diverse, the world is more interconnected and there is a more critical and sceptical attitude to all public services including the police. Where once, the police could count on largely uncritical support from certain sections of the media and the wider public, they actually face criticism and at times hostility from their traditional supporters in the tabloid press. The organisational demands on the police have included a much more formalised involvement in partnership and interagency working. The focus of this volume is the challenges of policing and mental health. This is one area that highlights these developments. Policing has been subject to an unusual period of austerity – particularly as it was imposed by Conservative-led administrations.

The PEQF seeks to professionalise police education and training so that officers can meet the policing challenges of the 21st century. One of the ongoing challenges that policing faces is the question of accountability and legitimacy. Since its creation in the 1820s, modern policing has always impact differentially on groups in society. The Peelian principles of equal treatment for all and so on were far removed from the reality. Vitale (2017) argues that policing as currently constituted cannot possibly meet the challenges of ensuring the safety of citizens while complying with modern standards of practice and accountability. The Black Lives Matters movement has focused a renewed spotlight on the area of race. The death of George Floyd in 2020 led to wider debates about the nature of the police function in societies that were increasing unequal. These debates have occurred in a slightly different form in the UK. Floyd's death led to protests across the world with many organisations, including my own university and police forces, making public statements about their commitment to tackling racism. The history of the police in creating and maintaining racist structures was also part of this debate. Any analysis of police legitimacy has to consider and recognise the long shadow that such a history casts.

There have been any number of attempts to reform the policing of marginalised communities or groups. However, to successfully achieve these laudable goals a much more nuanced understanding of structural inequality is required. Pickett and Wilkinson (2009) demonstrated that crime rates and a number of other social harms are high in more unequal societies. Britain was a more equal society in the mid-1970s before the Thatcherite revolution. We should not be surprised that those who suffer most from discriminatory forms of policing, experience the greatest discrimination in other areas such as education, health and employment. The solution to these issues and the creation of safer communities requires investment in services – housing, health, education and employment. This is not to suggest that the police forces and individual officers are not in a position to make a difference or cannot act more effectively in the interests of marginalised and vulnerable people. It is rather to recognise the impact of decades of increasingly deeply embedded inequality, exacerbated by ten years of austerity.

Loader (2016) concludes his outline of new Peelian principles with the recognition that policing is a public good. The public is much more prepared to question police professionalism both in the general sense but also at the individual operational level. The new forms of political oversight of the police – most importantly the Police and Crime Commissioner role – are poorly understood and there are very low turnouts in election. The role has not reinvigorated public confidence. The political and operational demands on the police have become more complex in a period where they have often become less visible to the public. Policing requires more specialist knowledge in several areas. Some key skills such as communication skills remain vital in the role. However, the challenges of modern policing require that the profession develops a more diverse workforce that reflects the communities that they serve. There needs to be a commitment to ethical individual and organisational behaviour that seeks to keep the use of coercive force to a minimum. Finally, new systems of democratic accountability need to be developed.

Further reading

Grieve, J.D.G. (2015) Historical perspective: British policing and the democratic ideal, in P. Wankhade and D. Weir (eds) *Police services leadership and management perspectives*. London Springer, pp 15–26.

Loader, I. (2013) *Why do the police matter? Beyond the myth of crime-fighting*. In J. Brown (ed) *The future of policing*. London: Routledge, 40–51.

Loader, I. (2016) In search of civic policing: recasting the 'Peelian' principles. *Criminal Law and Philosophy*, 10(3), 427–440.

Loftus, B. (2010) Police occupational culture: classic themes altered times. *Policing and Society*, 20(1), 1–20.

McDaniel, J., Moss, K. and Pease, K. (eds) (2020) *Policing and mental health: theory, policy and practice*. Abingdon: Routledge.

Punch, M. (1979) The secret social service. In S. Holdaway (ed), *The British police*. London: Hodder and Stoughton.

Vitale, A.S. (2017) *The end of policing*. London Verso Books.

2

Mental health and mental illness: key themes and perspectives

Introduction

This chapter provides a brief overview of some of the key debates and policy developments in the mental health field. The aim here is to provide an overview of debates in this area and contextualise the potential role of the police mental health work. Themes such as the experience of service users, the stigma attached to mental illness, and the failures to develop fully funded community-based services are examined throughout this volume. The chapter begins with a discussion of models of mental illness, and then explores the stigma attached to mental illness before examining social models of mental illness and considering the impact of social inequality on the experience of mental illness. The chapter then explores the development of community care. The final section examines relevant policy and legislation in the mental health field.

Models of mental health and illness

Mental illness is an area of ongoing controversy and debate. The history of the assessment and treatment of mental illness is scarred with examples of abuse carried out in the name of the enlightened relief of suffering and distress. Scull (2014), in outlining the cultural shifts and developments of new treatment, shows that societies have inflicted a range of indignities and physical abuse on individuals all in the name of therapy. There is a danger of thinking that this is history, interesting but of little relevance to modern mental health services that are based on core values such as dignity and respect. While not wanting to deny progress, it is important to recognise that these issues have not been fully resolved. One of the drivers of the Wessley review into the Mental Health Act (MHA) was the overuse of compulsory powers. Mental health is one of the few areas of medicine where doctors can treat individuals against their will. This generates huge ethical issues. In the context of policing, powers under 136 MHA allow non medically qualified professionals to detain a person on the basis of concerns about their mental state. As a society, we consider this is an appropriate and proportionate power. There is really little wider debate about these issues.

The stigma attached to mental illness is, in part, generated by the potential use of compulsory powers.

Any model of mental health and illness has to face the fundamental question of definition. Who defines what is regarded as illness and health has a profound impact on the individuals who are regarded as 'ill'. The impacts can be seen in the social stigma attached to illness. There are also potential impacts in public forums such as the courts. The MHA gives police officers specific powers to intervene in certain situations where an individual is experiencing a mental health crisis. The World Health Organization (WHO) defines mental health as 'a state of wellbeing in which the individual realizes his or her own abilities, can cope with the normal stresses of life, can work productively and fruitfully, and is able to make a contribution to his or her community'. There are some potential difficulties with this definition, for example, the emphasis on work and making a contribution to the community. However, this broad definition does emphasise that health should be viewed as more than absence of illness.

In very broad terms, it is possible to identify two main models of mental illness – medical (or disease) and social models. There is now a much wider recognition of the importance of the role of social determinants of mental illness and acceptance of the role they play in the generation of mental distress but also the experience of mental health services. Pickett and Wilkinson (2009) highlighted the wider impacts of inequality including in the area of mental health. The wider acceptance of a need to recognise the impact of social factors is due, in part, to the influence of 'critical psychiatry'. Critical psychiatry approaches (Cummins, 2017) question the power of the psychiatric profession and the scientific neutrality of diagnosis. There is an increasing recognition that the social/medical model division is reductive and redundant. There is a complex interplay between a range of factors – including social and biological ones. This approach leads to the development of a social investment model to reduce the occurrence of mental health problems but also to minimise their impact (Karban, 2016).

The medical model

The medical model uses the wider disease approach to the field of mental illness. This approach is based on identification and classification and then applying appropriate treatment options. Psychiatrists undergo specialist training which equips them with the skills and knowledge to enable them to make diagnosis. Diagnosis indicates not only the prognosis but also the best course of treatment. The major symptoms of severe mental illness such as hallucinatory experiences, low mood and suicidal thoughts can be traced to a physical cause. This causes include lesions in the brain or a chemical imbalance. This model is one that exists across medicine. The model assumes consistency of diagnosis – that is, psychiatrists are likely to agree on a diagnosis and proposed course of treatment. The model puts psychiatrists in a powerful position as they have the knowledge and expertise required to make these decisions. In addition, it establishes a paternalistic relationship between the doctors and patients.

The Mental State Examination

Police officers work alongside a range of mental health professionals. It is important that they recognise the ways that professional colleagues will approach these issues. It is important that police officers are aware of the way that other disciplines process or assess the importance of information. The Mental State Examination (MSE) is the standard assessment process used by psychiatrists. A psychiatrist will consider the following areas when carrying out a MSE:

- appearance
- mood – subjective and objective assessment
- thoughts
- speech
- behaviour
- drug/alcohol use
- forensic history
- family history

In the MSE, one can see how these areas are potentially subjective. How do we assess someone's appearance and what are the implications of this? Psychiatry is a middle-class profession. Doctors who are not originally from these backgrounds as part of their professional training develop a set of knowledge, skills and attitudes – in Bourdieu's (1998) terms, a 'habitus'. This creates a prism through which they see the world and their patients. This is not, of course, limited to psychiatrists; it is true of all professions and groups. There is an inbuilt danger of cultural misunderstanding or confusion as the result of class, race and gender differences. The disease model has at its core an assumption of medical objectivity. The supporters of the disease model highlight the extent of progress that has been made in research into specific mental health problems. Developments such as the Human Genome Project increase the hope there will be a medical breakthrough that will unlock the ongoing mystery of mental illness.

Critical psychiatry

The rise and expansion of the Diagnostic and Statistical Manual of Mental Disorders (DSM) is one sign of this. The increased dominance of bio-psychiatry was in part a response to the success of the radical critics of psychiatry such as Szasz, Foucault, Fanon and Laing (Cummins, 2017). There are a range of critical approaches to psychiatry. What they have in common is that they question the scientific rigour of diagnoses such as schizophrenia and the role of psychiatry as a form of social control. Psychiatrists struggled with the notion that they could be anything other than humanitarians concerned with relieving suffering (Ignatieff, 1985). The 1960s and 1970s saw the emergence of a school of radical criticism of the practices of institutionalised psychiatry. This critique was the work of scholars and activists from a range of backgrounds. The terms *anti-psychiatry* or, more recently, *critical psychiatry* are used to describe the work of thinkers such as Laing, Szasz, Foucault, Goffman and Fanon, who presented a radical critique of the scientific basis and institutions of modern psychiatry (Cummins, 2017). The views of this group were so diverse that it would be incorrect to think of critical psychiatry as a school. It is, perhaps, more useful to see it as a critical perspective. Laing, Szasz and Fanon were all psychiatrists but, aside from that, had little in common intellectually or politically. Laing and Szasz, while both suspicious of the role of the state, came from opposite ends of the political spectrum. Laing was a representative of the radical 1960s counterculture, Szasz an anti-statist libertarian. Fanon was a radical critical political theorist and anti-colonial activist. Thus, anti-psychiatry is a perspective that encompasses a number of wider political positions.

For Scull (2011), critical psychiatry was confused and often contradictory. In this period, psychiatry became a site for wider debates about the role of the state, the rights of marginalised groups and civil rights of those subject to compulsory detention. *The Bell Jar* (Plath, 2008) and *One Flew Over the Cuckoo's Nest* (Kesey, 2005) are two of the most popular and widely read modern American novels. Published in the early 1960s, they both explore the experiences of psychiatric patients. Kesey uses the psychiatric ward as a metaphor for the exploitative nature of modern capitalism. *The Bell Jar* examines the impact of social pressures on modern women. The position of psychiatry as a site of particular interest for the social sciences is demonstrated by the fact that major figures such as Foucault and Goffman produced work in this field.

In examining the huge range of work that goes to make up the critical perspective, it is possible to identify key themes:

• psychiatry lacks scientific rigour;
• psychiatric diagnosis is an act of social control or marginalisation;
• institutionalised psychiatry is dehumanising and abusive; and
• psychiatry is overly reliant on compulsory treatment. (Cummins, 2017)

Bentall (2004) presents a two-pronged attack on the medical model of mental illness. The first is the scientific validity of diagnoses such as schizophrenia and bipolar disorder. It is argued that there is much more of an overlap between symptoms in these broad areas of mental health diagnosis. One of the most stigmatising aspects of this approach to severe mental illness is to see diagnosis as destiny. The destiny here is negative experiences of admission to hospital, lack of employment opportunities and social marginalisation. Bentall (2004) counters this by highlighting that large numbers of people are able to live productive lives and make a positive contribution to society despite experiencing symptoms of severe psychiatric illness. There is an international network of people who hear voices but approach this is in a completely different way to seeing it as a symptom of illness (Intervoice, nd).

Critical approaches played a clear role in the development of the policy of deinstitutionalisation (Cummins, 2017, 2020b). The perspectives shifted the focus from individual illness and symptomology to a range of social, cultural and environmental factors that have role in or increase the likelihood of the development of mental health problems. These include factors such as growing up in poverty, migration and being a member of an ethnic minority, childhood sexual and physical abuse. A narrow biomedical approach individualises all problems (Bentall, 2016).

Varese et al's (2012) meta-analysis indicates that these childhood adversities increase the risk of psychosis by a factor of three. Those who experienced multiple traumatic events were at greater risk. Bentall (2016) argues that:

> To make matters worse, research shows that an exclusively biological approach tends to increase the stigma associated with mental illness. The more that ordinary people think of mental illness as a genetically determined brain disease, and the less they recognise it to be a reaction to unfortunate circumstances, the more they shun psychiatric patients. An exclusively biological approach makes it all too easy to believe that human beings fall into two subspecies: the mentally well and the mentally ill.

Critical perspectives on the use of drugs in psychiatry

The discovery of the major tranquilisers in the 1950s was one of the factors in the development of deinstitutionalisation. The early psychiatric drugs had damaging side effects such as tardive dyskinesia – where patients developed Parkinson's like symptoms. Critics of their use came to see them as a means of managing patients with the so-called 'chemical cosh' rather than therapeutic interventions (Braslow, 1997). Moncrieff (2004) outlines the way that certain drugs, Prozac being an example, have been so widely prescribed that they are well known and have become part of the cultural landscape. One of the most fundamental criticisms of the increase in the use of drug treatments is the use of medication in cases involving children and young people. For example, there has been a huge increase in prescriptions for Ritalin – a treatment for attention deficit hyperactivity disorder (ADHD). In 2010, 661,000 were dispensed compared with 359,100 in 2004 (Boffey, 2015). It is important to remember that these are prescriptions that are given to children. This is, in itself, a concern. In addition, many would see this as an example of the much broader trend of the medicalisation of social or behavioural problems.

Moncrieff (2004) concludes that:

> This increase in use of prescribed drugs has been achieved firstly by extending the boundaries of well recognised conditions like depression and psychosis. Secondly, lesser known disorders such as panic disorder and social phobia have been publicised, and thirdly, drug treatment has started to colonise areas where it was previously thought to be unhelpful such as substance misuse and personality disorder.

Behavioural models

The development of major tranquilisers for the treatment of mental illness has meant that the behaviourist approach, most closely associated with Skinner (2002, 2012), is not as popular. Skinner believed that behaviour was learnt or 'conditioned'. In most cases, through either punishment or reward we learn behaviour that enables us to successfully adapt to society. Skinner's (2002, 2012) work suggested that rewarding good behaviour was the most effective way to bring about change. Alongside this, there should be sanctions for poor or inappropriate behaviour. This is a model that is, perhaps, most common in advice to parents. In terms of mental illness, such behaviours are termed maladaptive. These maladaptive behaviours may reinforce original symptoms. For example, if you have a fear of certain social situations you will avoid them. Avoiding them increases anxiety about being in that situation in future. Behaviourist models would not seek to examine the original causes of this anxiety – they would seek to change the behaviour. Behaviourism is at the root of some of the more shameful abuses that scar psychiatry such as aversion therapy to 'cure' gay men (Dickinson, 2014).

Behaviourist ideas are at the root of patient contracts. Examples might include regular attendees at accident and emergency departments or frequent callers to the emergency services who are either banned from such services or charged with offences to try and change the behaviour. The main difficult with this approach is that such contracts are difficult to enforce consistently by all staff and agencies. Second, they do not address the underlying causes of the distress that an individual is experiencing.

Cognitive models

Cognitive approaches to mental ill health have become increasingly popular. The model was developed from Beck's (1976) treatment of depression. The growth in the use of cognitive behavioural therapy (CBT) in mental health settings is the clearest evidence of the influence of these approaches. The cognitive approach sees disordered thinking as the cause of mental ill health. In contrast to behaviourist approaches, the focus is very much on the impact of thinking and how that can distort perspectives. Cognitive models are based on a premise that our view of the world is shaped by our perceptions. We respond to situations, events and people through a series of filters. We create these filters. At the same time, we look for evidence that will support or confirm our view of the world. For example, if you experience chronically low self-esteem, this will act as a filter through which you make judgements about your own life and achievements. In so doing, you will focus on the examples or situations that provide evidence of your own failure and generalise from them.

The following are examples patterns of thinking that CBT or other cognitive approaches would seek to change:

- *Arbitrary thinking*: reaching a conclusion without evidence to support it.
- *Selective abstraction*: reaching a conclusion for the whole experience on the basis of this one aspect.
- *Overgeneralisation*: using an incident to reach generalised conclusions.
- *Evaluation*: overvaluing the significance or importance of an event.
- *Personalisation*: blaming oneself for external events when there is no basis for making such a connection.
- *Absolute and binary thinking*: deciding that experiences are either wholly positive or negative and placing yourself in the most extreme negative category.

CBT, as noted, has its roots in the treatment of depressive illness. However, its use as a treatment has been extended to other disorders including substance abuse, bipolar disorder, personality disorders, and anorexia nervosa (Beck, 1997). It has also been used alongside medication in the treatment of psychotic illnesses (Butler et al, 2006). There are many positive aspects to these approaches. However, critics note that they do not address the wider structural factors that leave people marginalised – so-called faulty models of thinking may be realistic depending on individual circumstances.

Mental health and inequality

There is an increasing body of research that demonstrates the link between mental ill health and inequality. The Marmot Review (2010) is the most comprehensive review of these issues. It highlighted that social inequality is linked to the experience of mental health problems in complex ways. Poverty and social disadvantage are linked to increased levels of depression and anxiety, psychosis, self-harm and suicide. These links are complex but the Marmot Review emphasised that the roots of these poor mental health outcomes begin in childhood and adolescence. They then widen across the life course. The factors that cause these outcomes are a range of multiple, interrelated forms of social disadvantage including low educational attainment, living in poverty or on a low income, precarious forms of employment and living in poor or insecure housing. These factors are widely recognised as the social determinants of health. This approach moves away from a perspective that pathologises individuals and groups to examine structural patterns of disadvantage (Karban, 2016). This approach recognises that mental ill health is an individual experience while recognising that structural change is required to tackle underlying causes. This structural analysis recognises that factors such as poor housing and education disproportionately affect certain groups, including people from Black, Asian and Minority Ethnic (BAME) backgrounds. These can be potentially compounded by inequalities in mental health and the provision of services. One of the reasons for the Wessley Review of the MHA was overgoing concerns about the hugely negative experiences of Black people within mental health services. There are other areas too, for example, austerity policies had a disproportionate impact on mental health (Cummins, 2018a, 2018b). There is a pincer effect here. Austerity led to increases in precarity and reduced welfare benefits (apart from pensions). These changes added to the stresses of the lives of the most vulnerable. At the same time, the services available to support people faced cuts and retrenchment meaning that they were increasingly stretched. Policies such as the so-called bedroom tax, Work Capability Assessments and more punitive welfare systems clearly disproportionately impact on the most vulnerable. There is emerging qualitative and quantitative evidence to suggest that the rollout of Universal Credit (UC) is associated with worse mental health problems, including suicidal thoughts (Cummins, 2018a, 2018b).

Stigma

Despite huge changes in social and cultural attitudes, there is still a stigma attached to mental illness. This remains the case despite the fact that high profile individuals including celebrities, even royalty, are much more open and prepared to discuss their own experiences of mental ill health. Stigma is a sociological concept as well as set of emotions and experiences. The sociologist Ervin Goffman wrote two hugely influential texts related to the experience of mental illness. The first, *Asylums* (1961), was based on the ethnographic research that he undertook at a large psychiatric hospital. In *Asylums*, Goffman identified the essentially dehumanising and abusive nature of the long stay state asylum system. The work became a key text for those arguing for the policy that came to be known as deinstitutionalisation – that is, the closure of such institutions (Cummins, 2020b). Goffman published *Stigma: notes on a spoiled identity* (1963) after his work on asylums. However, the two can be read as two halves of the same argument. The work on stigma forms a backdrop to the way that total institutions function in the creation and maintenance of the social ostracism of the mentally ill. In Ancient Greece, stigma were the marks that were cut or burned into the body of those who had transgressed the laws and morals of the time. Stigma is socially constructed. It is relational. People with mental health problems face a series of negative and discriminatory attitudes. This is not just about social attitudes or being the subject of offensive humour. People with mental health problems face ongoing discrimination in areas such as employment and housing. This remains the case despite the fact that the Equality Act (2010) recognises mental ill health as a protected characteristic.

Stigma is a very powerful force. He argues that we are often complicit in the maintenance of stigmatised status of individuals and groups. There are two potential stages to the normative process of stigmatisation – the *discreditable* and the *discredited*. The attribute that is seen as stigmatising is not necessarily apparent or visible. Individuals are aware that there is a potential reaction from others if they disclose that they are experience a stigmatising condition. Mental illness is a clear example. It is, therefore, possible that an individual might keep this hidden. Goffman termed this 'passing'. 'Passing' carries with it the possibility that the individual will be unintentionally or deliberately outed. Individuals take steps to prevent this because they fear the consequences. It might be possible to suggest that the changes in the nearly 60 years since Goffman published his influential work mean that the stigma attached to mental illness has significantly reduced. This is a complex debate. There has undoubtedly been progress in some areas. However, it is also the case that elements of the organisational culture that Goffman identified remain.

Criticisms of celebrity led stigma campaigns (Tyler, 2020) argue that they ignore the political and social context which generates feelings of mental distress – what Tyler (2020) terms the 'political economy of stigma'. There is a clear social gradient in the experience of mental illness (Marmot, 2010; Karban, 2016; Cummins, 2018b). This is not to deny the pain and mental anguish that high profile individuals feel. It is rather to emphasise the social determinants of mental health. It is good to talk and be more open and honest about experiences of mental distress. However, that is not enough, real social change is required to tackle the underlying causes. One of the most significant developments in modern rich societies is that despite material progress rates of mental distress seem to be increasing. James (2008) terms this 'affluenza' – a form of modern angst caused by a combination of work pressures and consumerism. For example in the period 2005–2015, there was a doubling in antidepressant prescriptions. In 2015, the total was 31.6 million more than in 2005. It had increased by 3.9 million, or 6.8 per cent, from 2014 (Meikle, 2015). Rich Western societies are consuming larger and larger quantities of these drugs. We might add to this the rates of alcohol and substance misuse as individuals use these to cope with the pressures of modern life or block out experiences of trauma.

Critical perspectives on psychiatry also highlight the relationship between drug manufacturers and medicine (Moncrieff, 2004). These criticisms are not limited to psychiatry. Moncrieff (2004) summarises a series of concerns in this field. Drug companies spend a great deal of money on advertising and hospitality to convince doctors and funding bodies to use their products in clinical practice. This, in itself, is a concern. In addition, the whole thrust here is that the solution to personal and other problems can be found in a pill that can be taken every day. Moncrieff (2004) makes the very important point that medication offers a simple, complete and technical solution to a range of complex social and personal problems. In so doing it, it marginalises the real causes of these issues such as the impact of interpersonal violence or the long-term effect of living in poverty. This is something of a caricature of the medical approach but it is a criticism that needs to be taken seriously. Medication can be part of a response but it cannot not be the only solution.

Radical critics of the drug industry argue that it pushes a narrow biomedical approach to further its own economic interests. As in any market, drug companies need to develop areas of growth and create new demands for their products. The critical perspective argues that this leads to the medicalisation of essentially social issues. The result is the expansion of psychiatric medicine into social and personal relationships in a way that did not exist previously. Thus, shyness becomes *social anxiety disorder*. One can be concerned about these trends but an element of caution is required. It is far too easy to mock such moves without taking account of the real impact that, for example, social anxiety has on the people who experience it. Psychiatry is an important area for the pharmaceutical industry because it seems possible to both create new syndromes and offer the cure to them at the same time.

Mental health policy and legislation

This section will outline the development of community care. It will then consider other relevant mental health and safeguarding policies and legislation. Specific police powers under sections 135 and 136 of the MHA as well as the protections for vulnerable adults under the Police and Criminal Evidence Act (PACE) will be examined in detail in the next chapter.

Deinstitutionalisation and the development of community care

Deinstitutionalisation is the term that is used for the policy of closing the long stay mental health hospitals. In theory, the closure of these institutions was meant to lead to the development of community-based mental health services. Community care is a term that rarely features in contemporary debates about mental health policy (Cummins, 2020b). This is partly because there is no real call for a return to the institutionalised forms of psychiatric care that they represented. It does not mean that the progressive vision of community care has been realised. Far from it, the police and wider CJS involvement in mental health systems is one example of many that demonstrate this. Deinstitutionalisation has become the accepted model of mental health delivery. It is seen as a measure of progress that it is adopted as an approach (Cummins, 2020b).

Enoch Powell's Water Tower Speech (1961) can be regarded as the start of the policy of community care in England and Wales. In this speech, Powell (not exactly a liberal or progressive) argued that developments in medication would mean that the need for long stay institutional care would be removed. It would be naïve to assume that this was the only reason for the reduction of community care. As in all areas, policy development in this field is messy and complex. Progressive values, new treatments and fiscal pressures combine to make deinstitutionalisation an attractive policy option. The balance between these three main elements varies across settings and time periods (Cummins, 2020c). By the 1980s, the pressures on the asylum regimes meant that they were no longer sustainable. Community care was a policy that was adapted across a range of areas. However, it came to be most closely associated with mental health policy. The failure to develop properly funded and resourced mental health services meant that the term took on such negative associations that it disappeared from public discourse. More recent research, such as Parsons (2018), have emphasised the importance of examining how these factors play out locally. In addition, Parsons (2018) highlights the important roles that individuals can play in the implementation of broad national policies. One of the ironies of the community care policy is that, on the whole, it is associated with progressive values and claims, but in the UK, its introduction was largely overseen by Conservatives committed to a reduction in the welfare state.

The drive towards community care was heavily influenced by the challenge to the conditions in the institutions. There are many strands of thought within this movement which succeeded in making the treatment of mental illness in its coercive institutionalised form an issue of human rights. Radical theorists such as Basaglia (Foot, 2015) in Italy used their critique of mental health services as part of a wider attack on capitalism. The critics of institutionalised psychiatry of the late 1950s and early 1960s highlighted the way that it excluded individuals – physically but also socially and legally. Patients in long stay institutions were denied the full rights of citizenship. In addition, the conditions in these institutions were often very poor indeed. Therefore, services need to be able to intervene at an early stage to provide support. One of the great achievements of Basaglia and other radical critics of psychiatry and the asylum as an institution was that they were able to bring the totally unacceptable and abusive practices of the asylum to the attention of a national and international public. This did this by successfully and properly recasting the issue of institutionalised psychiatric care as one of human rights. The core of the radical critique of psychiatry is the claim for the recognition of the dignity and thus the human rights of those who were abandoned in the asylums and similar institutions.

Community care

Community care as a policy has been tainted by an association with the failures that took place in the late 1980s and early 1990s. Community care as a policy was not only implemented in the field mental health field. However, it is mostly closely associated with mental health. This was emphasised by negative media coverage and a series of inquiries into homicides committed by people with serious mental illness. These failings undermined wider support for the policy but also led to calls for reform of the MHA, including the introduction of Community Treatment Orders (CTOs) (Cummins, 2020b). This section will briefly examine these areas. To understand the current position in mental health services, it is important to have an understanding of their history and development. The failings of community care led to a shift towards more managerialist approaches to the delivery of services with an increased focus on audit, professional accountability and, in its broadest sense, surveillance.

Deinstitutionalisation was meant to replace the discredited asylums with a range of community-based services. The asylum was a closed and hidden institution, and this was one of the reasons that abuse could occur (Philo, 1987; Scull, 1987). Community care was never able to establish inclusive services. Moon (2000) notes that the physical separation of the asylum continued into the community. The optimistic vision of well-resourced community mental health services that were able to support people in crisis has never materialised. Instead, those with the most complex needs were often living in the poorest neighbourhoods, poor quality supported housing, or on the streets or in the prison system (Singleton et al, 1998; Moon, 2000; Wolff, 2005). These developments have been termed 'transinstitutionalisation'.

In 1998, when he introduced the document *Modernising mental health services* (Department of Health, 1998), Frank Dobson announced that 'community care has failed'. This policy paper outlines the organisational and other failings of mental health policy in the previous 20 years. The paper's introduction recognised services were underfunded and suffered from organisational issues – health and social work teams did not always cover the same patch. Marking a noticeable shift in attitudes, *Modernising mental health services* (Department of Health, 1998) argued that mental health policy had shifted so that the rights of individuals took precedence over concerns of their friends and families and the protection of the wider community. This statement of New Labour policy echoed many of the themes that were evident in a series of inquiries into failure in community care services (Ritchie et al, 1994; Blom-Cooper et al, 1995). The focus of these inquiries was on individual cases and the failings of agencies. They also examined the legislative and policy framework, seeking solutions in proposing new legislation or forms of service audit such as the Care Programme Approach (CPA), Supervised Discharge and Supervision Registers. Apart from the CPA, these were short-lived policies. They were steps on the way to the introduction of CTOs, which finally occurred with the reform of the MHA in 2007.

The media portrayal of community care was a consistent factor in undermining attempts to create a popular base for support of the policy. In the early 1990s, the media focused on a series of violent offences, particularly homicides, committed by individuals in contact with mental health services. Cohen's (1972) notion of a 'moral panic' is concerned with the ways that the media, particularly the press and later TV, produce a representation of events. A moral panic does not just appear. There is some basis for the concerns raised. The moral panic refers to the reaction of the authorities. One of the key features of the moral panic is the creation of the figure of the modern folk devil. Modern folk devils have included teddy boys, mods, punk rockers, muggers and paedophiles. These are figures who are 'discovered' or created by media outlets and seen as posing some sort of existential threat to society. Cummins (2012) has shown that in the history of community care, the folk devil was the 'schizophrenic'. There was an intersection between race and class here as the media portrayals of community care focused on a series of cases involving young working-class Black men – usually convicted of a violent crime. Cummins (2010) uses the most high profile inquiry of the period – the *Ritchie inquiry into the care and treatment of Christopher Clunis* (Ritchie et al, 1994) – to illustrate this point. Cross (2010) notes that the continuing representations of the mad emphasise physicality – size, uncontrollable hair – as signifiers of irrationality. They also intersect with racist stereotyping of Black men.

The argument here is not that the media should not report violent crimes committed by people with serious mental health problems. It is that the focus and structure of this report did not contextualise these appalling incidents in terms of the pressures on mental health services. A close reading of the Ritchie Inquiry reveals examples of poor practice – there are some examples of excellent practice as well. The inquiry also shows that mental health services were stretched beyond belief in London in the early 1990s. The media reporting of these cases led to calls 'for something to be done'. It is easier and quicker to introduce policies such as registers that list people see at risk or who might be violent when unwell. It is more expensive and complex to invest in services and change organisational working cultures. The asylums could not be rebuilt but new forms of surveillance emerged culminating in the introduction of CTOs (Cummins, 2020a).

This section will briefly discuss the main provisions of the Mental Capacity Act (MCA) (2005) and the MHA (2007). The section also includes a brief discussion of the background to the Wessley Review of the MHA. Table 2.1 outlines the most relevant legislation in the mental health field. Police officers are not mental health nurses, social workers or lawyers but they need a working knowledge of this legislation.

The Mental Health Act (2007)

The MHA created the legal framework that governs the assessment and admission to hospital of individuals experiencing mental health problems. The use of coercion is one of the most controversial areas in psychiatry. Critics such as Szmukler (2018) argue that the current legislation is outdated and inherently discriminatory. The Wessley Review of the MHA has proposed a rights-based approach. Working in mental health services inevitably means that one has to confront the ethical issues raised by the use of compulsory powers. It is also important to remember that professionals will be working with service users, who have been subject to these powers, often in traumatising fashion. In terms of the policing role, police officers can be called to support Approved Mental Health Professionals (AMHPs) and execute a section 135 MHA warrant. The police will also be involved when patients who are detained under the MHA are reported missing from a mental health unit.

The Mental Health Act: assessment and formal admission to hospital

One of the overarching principles of the current MHA is the 'least restrictive' principle. This means that all steps should be taken to prevent hospital admission. If a patient – the MHA refers to patients throughout – is admitted to hospital it should be on a voluntary basis if possible. A patient

Table 2.1: Key policy and legislation (summary for police officers of key legislation and powers)

Policy/legislation	Key points
Mental Health Act	NHS *Guide to your rights* (easy read)
Mental Health Act Code of Practice	Code of Practice
Guidance from the College of Policing	College of Policing Guidance
Police, courts and prison	*Rethink mental illness* – guide for those in contact with CJS
Section 2 MHA	• Admission for assessment • Lasts up to 28 days • It cannot be renewed
Section 3 MHA	• Admission for assessment • Lasts up to 28 days • It can be renewed • Patients entitled to section 117 aftercare
Section 25 MHA – CTOs	• Conditions placed on section 3 patients when they are discharged • Patients can be recalled to hospital if they do not comply
Section 117 MHA	• Duty on health and social services to support patients who have been detained under section 3 • Individuals cannot be charged for services provided under section 117
Section 135 MHA – warrant	• AMHP can apply to a magistrate's court for a warrant to enter a person's home • MH professionals must have concerns that a person is being ill-treated or is unable to care for themselves • Police must be accompanied by AMHP and a registered medical practitioner to execute the warrant • MHA is carried out either at the home or a place of safety
Section 135 MHA – missing	• A warrant can be obtained from the magistrate's court if a detained person is missing or AWOL • Warrant can only be obtained if all reasonable attempts to contact the patient have been unsuccessful
Section 136 MHA – police power	• Police power • Used in circumstances where there are concerns that a person has a mental disorder and they are putting themselves or others at risk • Police officer should consult a mental health professional before using section 136 power • MHA assessment has to be carried out

(continued)

Table 2.1: Key policy and legislation (summary for police officers of key legislation and powers) (continued)

Policy/legislation	Key points
Section 136 MHA – place of safety	A place of safety can be: • a hospital – usually a section 136 suite; • a care home; • a police station – only in exceptional circumstances; • your or someone else's home or room; • other suitable premises where the manager of those premises agrees. Police stations cannot be used for under 18s in any circumstances.
PACE – vulnerable groups	• All juveniles • Adults with a learning disability • Adults with a mental health problem
PACE – the role of the AA	• Vulnerable detained persons must be interviewed with an AA present • NAAN guidance and advice

who is detained under the MHA should be discharged from that section at the earliest opportunity. Patients who are detained should be in the least restrictive conditions.

The AMHP role was created by the reform of the Mental Health Act in 2007. AMHPs replaced the Approved Social Workers but carry out essentially the same role. The major change was that the role is not now limited to social workers. The majority of AMHPs are from a social work background. The role of the AMHP is outlined in the MHA Code of Practice (DH, 2008). The AMHP has overall responsibility for the coordination of assessments under the MHA. This can involve a range of tasks, potentially involving: arranging two doctors to carry out the required medical assessments; making a decision as to whether police support is required; and attending the Magistrates Court to obtain a warrant under section 135 MHA

The MHA, unlike other legislation, does not include any mention of age. This is unusual as, in other areas, there will be often be separate legislation for adults and children. In addition to the MHA, a Code of Practice is issued. The two need to be taken together as they establish the legal and policy framework.

For both sections 2 and 3, the assessment involves:

- an AMHP;
- a section 12 MHA approved doctor – a consultant psychiatrist or a registrar; and
- a registered medical practitioner, usually the GP of the person being assessed.

There are two elements to any MHA assessment. The first is whether the person is suffering from a mental disorder within the meaning of the Act. The second question for all involved is whether there are any other ways of addressing the current crisis situation. While acknowledging that a compulsory admission to hospital is sometimes the only realistic intervention, it is important to emphasise that it should be a last resort. Professionals making these difficult decisions should make them on the basis that all community-based options have been explored and are not able to meet the person's needs and that the patient's own health or safety are at risk, or that there is a need to protect other people.

Key terms in the Mental Health Act (2007)
Definition of mental disorder

The reform of the MHA in 2007 included a new definition of mental disorder which is now defined as 'any disorder or disability of mind'. Substance misuse is not classified as a disorder under the MHA. A person with a learning disability can only be subject to the provisions of the MHA if their behaviour is additionally considered abnormally aggressive or seriously irresponsible.

Nearest Relative

Section 26 of the MHA defines who someone's Nearest Relative (NR) is. This is an important role and it is one where the law is very prescriptive. NRs should be consulted before a section 3 assessment and can object to one being carried out.

Sections of the MHA
Section 2

- Admission for assessment.
- Lasts for a period of up to 28 days.
- Section 2 cannot be renewed.
- During the 28-day period, staff should develop a plan for ongoing treatment.
- The least restrictive principle means that a decision about whether to seek a further period of detention under section 3 should be made as soon as feasible.
- Right of appeal to the Hospital Managers and the Mental Health Tribunal.
- Legal aid is available for Mental Health Review Tribunals.
- Patients have the right to support from an Independent Mental Health Advocate (IHMA).

Section 3

- Admission for treatment.
- Nearest relative must be consulted.
- Lasts for a period of up to six months.
- It can be renewed for a period of six months and then for 12 months.
- Right of appeal to the Hospital Managers and the Mental Health Tribunal.
- Patients detained under section 3 are entitled to Section 117 MHA aftercare.
- Legal aid is available for Mental Health Review Tribunals.
- Patients have the right to support from a IHMA.

Section 5(2)

- Emergency section – doctor's power.
- If staff are concerned about the health of a voluntary patient, this section allows for an emergency detention for a period of up to 72 hours.
- During this period, a MHA assessment with view to an admission under section 2 or 3 must be completed.

Section 25 MHA Supervised Community Treatment Orders

CTOs were one of the key responses to the failings of community care in the 1990s. Versions of CTOs were suggested in various inquiries. The reform of the MHA was a tortuous process and there is not space to explore it here. The arguments in favour of CTOs are based on two key claims. The first is that there is a group of patients who are repeatedly detained under the MHA. The major factor in these repeat detentions is the failure to comply with medication. The second claim is that within this cohort, there is a separate group of patients who pose a significant risk to themselves and others when they are unwell. CTOs would ensure compliance with medication and cooperation with other services, minimise risk and improve broader outcomes.

A CTO can be considered when a patient who has been detained under section 3 is being discharged from hospital. Conditions can be placed on the discharge. These might include:

- having to live in a certain place;
- being tested for alcohol or illegal drugs; and
- attending appointments for treatment.

The CTO introduced the power of recall to hospital if the responsible clinician has concerns that:

- the patient needs medical treatment in hospital for a mental disorder; and
- there would be risk of harm to the health or safety of the patients or of others.

The patient can be recalled for up to 72 hours where decisions are made about future treatment plans and support.

Section 117 MHA aftercare

Section 117 of the MHA provides that certain groups of patients who have been detained under the MHA are entitled to aftercare. The biggest group is those patients who have been detained under section 3. Patients cannot be charged for services provided under section 117 of the MHA.

Mental Health Review Tribunals (MHRT)

First tier tribunals in England hear appeals against compulsory admission. These tribunals comprise:

- a lawyer who chairs the hearing;
- a 'lay' member who is experienced in the area of mental health; and
- an independent psychiatrist, who examines the patient before the panel hearing.

The MHRT can decide that the grounds for detention no longer apply and the patient should be discharged.

Trends in the use of the Mental Health Act

The Mental Health Services Dataset (MHSDS) is the official source of national statistics on the use of the MHA. It is possible to identify trends in the overall use of the MHA. The rates of detention have been increasing over the past 15 years.

- There were 49,988 new detentions under the MHA in 2018/2019.
- Detention rates were higher for males (91.4 per 100,000 population) than females (83.2 per 100,000 population).
- Detention rates vary by age group:
  - 18–34: 128.9 detentions per 100,000 population;
  - 50–64: 89.0 per 100,000 population; and
  - 65+ age group: 98.1 per 100,000 population.
- Rates of detention are higher among BAME groups.

- Rate of detention for Black or Black British people in 2018/2019 was 306.8 detentions per 100,000 population.
- Rate of detention for White British people was 72.9 per 100,000 population.
- CTO use varies significantly by age and gender:
  - males: 11.2 per 100,000 population;
  - females: 6.1 per 100,000 population;
  - overall CTO use: 8.6 per 100,000 population for all age groups; and
  - CTO use highest in the 35–49 age group (15.3 known uses per 100,000 population versus 8.6 uses per 100,000 population for all age groups).
- Black or Black British people were more likely to be subject to CTOs – 53.8 uses per 100,000 population.
- Rate of CTOs for White British people was 6.4 uses per 100,000 population.

The Mental Capacity Act (2005)

The MCA provides a legal framework for the assessment of individual capacity. Capacity means having the ability to make a decision and to take actions. There is a presumption in favour of a capacity – that is, there has to be evidence to prove that an individual can be deemed to lack capacity. A person cannot be said to lack capacity simply because of an illness or disability.

Where individuals are deemed as lacking capacity to make a particular decision then those doing so on their behalf must act in their best interests. The MCA applies to anyone over the age of 16. A person's capacity may well fluctuate depending on their mental state or other factors.

Key principles that underpin the Mental Capacity Act (2005)

There are five key principles that underpin the MCA:

- presumption of capacity;
- support and assist people to make their own decisions;
- people can make unwise decisions;
- any decisions made for an individual who lacks capacity must be in their best interests; and
- least restrictive options should be chosen.

The important conclusions to draw here are:

- If an individual they can make a decision. Professionals cannot use the decision they make as evidence to show they lack capacity.
- People can make decisions that others might see as unwise, foolish or not in their best interests. This is part of being an adult.

Decisions about capacity

There is a two-stage test to decide whether an individual has the capacity to make a particular decision.

• Stage 1. Is there an impairment of or disturbance in the functioning of a person's mind or brain? If so:
• Stage 2. Is the impairment or disturbance sufficient that the person lacks the capacity to make a particular decision?

Lack of capacity

The MCA states that a person lacks capacity if one of the following applies:

A person cannot understand information given to them.

• They cannot retain that information long enough to be able to make the decision.
• They cannot weigh up the information available to make the decision.
• They cannot communicate their decision – this could be by talking, using sign language or even simple muscle movements.

Professionals have to demonstrate that they have made every effort to ascertain whether the person has capacity.

Advanced decision making

The MCA aims to enhance personal autonomy (Manthorpe et al, 2009). Part of the process of doing this was the creation of a new framework and roles where individuals wished to make advanced care and treatment decisions. The key roles in this framework are:

• Lasting Powers of Attorney (LPAs) – the MCA allows people over the age of 18 to formally appoint one or more people to look after their health, welfare and/or financial decisions.
• Court of Protection and Deputies – the MCA created a new court and a new public official to protect people who lack capacity and to supervise those making decisions on their behalf.
• The Public Guardian – the role of the Public Guardian is to protect people who lack capacity from abuse. The Public Guardian is supported by the Office of the Public Guardian (OPG).
• Independent mental capacity advocate (IMCA) – IMCAs are a statutory safeguard for people who lack capacity to make some important decisions.

This includes decisions about where the person lives and serious medical treatment when the person does not have family or friends who can represent them (Social Care Institute for Excellence, nd).

Deprivation of Liberty Safeguards

Article 5 of the Human Rights Act (HRA, 1998) – the right to liberty – states that 'everyone has the right to liberty and security of person. No one shall be deprived of his or her liberty [unless] in accordance with a procedure prescribed in law'. The MCA (2005) allows for the use of restraint where it is felt that this is neccessary to ensure the safety of the individual. The Supreme Court decided in the case known as *Cheshire West* that a person is deprived of their liberty if the following applies:

- they lack the capacity to consent to their care/treatment arrangements;
- are under continuous supervision and control; and
- are not free to leave.

The Deprivation of Liberty Safeguards (DOLs) can only be used if the person will be deprived of their liberty in a care home or hospital. Best Interest Assessors (BIAs) carry out an assessment role in overseeing the use of these powers.

The Care Act (2014)

The Care Act (2014) creates a new legal framework for how systems should seek to protect adults at risk of abuse or neglect. The Care Act (2014) section 1(1) placed a general duty on local authorities to promote the wellbeing of the individual. Slasberg and Beresford (2014) note that combined with guidance issued subsequent to the Act, any assessment must begin from 'the assumption that the individual is best placed to judge the individual's wellbeing'. The introduction of the Act also saw the introduction of the concept of a national 'minimum eligibility threshold'. This replaced the previous policy, Fair Access to Care Services (FACS) (Department of Health, 2002). The aim was to provide consistency and transparency in this area.

Adult safeguarding

Safeguarding can be viewed as the adult equivalent of child protection – that is, a system that is designed to protect individuals from abuse and neglect. The current system involves a range of agencies including health, social services and the police. It places duties on these agencies to work together to ensure that vulnerable adults are not neglected or abused but also that individuals are empowered to make meaningful choices about their lives. Safeguarding has to be more than a bureaucratic process. One criticism of current approaches is that the focus on procedures drains the system of values and a real commitment to individuals. There is a disconnect between policy statements and the practice on the ground. The fundamental principles of safeguarding are:

- Empowerment: people being supported and encouraged to make their own decisions and give informed consent.
- Prevention: it is better to take action before harm occurs.
- Proportionality: the least intrusive response appropriate to the risk presented.
- Protection: support and representation for those in greatest need.
- Partnership: local solutions through services working with their communities – communities have a part to play in preventing, detecting and reporting neglect and abuse.
- Accountability and transparency in safeguarding practice (Social Care Institute for Excellence, nd).

Safeguarding Adults Boards

Local Safeguarding Adults Boards (SABs) have an overall responsibility to lead adult safeguarding. The SABs have three core duties:

- develop and publish a strategic plan setting out how they will meet their objectives and how their member and partner agencies will contribute;
- publish an annual report detailing how effective their work has been; and
- commission safeguarding adults reviews (SARs) for any cases which meet the criteria for these. (Social Care Institute for Excellence, nd)

The SABs have to focus on a broad range of issues, including:

- the safety of people who use services in local health settings, including mental health;
- the safety of adults with care and support needs living in social housing;
- effective interventions with adults who self-neglect, for whatever reason;
- the quality of local care and support services;
- the effectiveness of prisons in safeguarding offenders; and
- making connections between adult safeguarding and domestic abuse. (Social Care Institute for Excellence, nd)

Conclusion

The next chapter will examine the police role in mental health work in more depth. It will also discuss the current pressures on police officers in this area. When Lord Adebowale (2013) described mental health work as 'core police business', he was highlighting both the organisational demands but also the fact that this is an issue that officers wherever they are based are likely to face on a daily basis. Mental health work is an area where police officers have to work in both formal and informal ways with colleagues from across a range of disciplines. It is, therefore, vital that officers have a working knowledge of policies and procedures in the mental health area but also the roles and responsibilities of other mental health professionals.

Further reading

Bentall, R. (2016) Mental illness is a result of misery, yet we still stigmatise it. *The Guardian.* Available at: https://www.theguardian.com/commentisfree/2016/feb/26/mental-illness-misery-childhood-traumas

College of Policing (2015) *Mental vulnerability and illness.* Available at: https://www.app.college.police.uk/app-content/mental-health/mental-vulnerability-and-illness/

Cummins, I. (2017) *Critical psychiatry: a biography.* Northwich: Critical Publishing.

Goffman, E. (2009) *Stigma: notes on the management of spoiled identity.* New York: Simon and Schuster.

Kesey, K. (2005) *One flew over the cuckoo's Nest.* London: Penguin.

Moncrieff, J. (2004) *Is psychiatry for sale: an examination of the influence of the pharmaceutical industry on academic and practical psychiatry.* Available at: http://www.critpsynet.freeuk.com/pharmaceuticalindustry.htm

Moon, G. (2000) Risk and protection: the discourse of confinement in contemporary mental health policy. *Health & Place,* 6(3), 239–250.

3

Policing, mental health and the criminal justice system

Introduction

This chapter will begin with a brief consideration of how mental health issues can affect decision making across the CJS. The chapter will then examine police powers under the MHA and the protections offered to vulnerable adults by PACE.

Table 3.1 outlines decision points in the CJS and relevant mental health policies.

Section 136 of the Mental Health Act (2007)

One of the most important areas that the police are involved in is responding to mental health emergencies. There are specific roles and powers for the police within the mental health field. These include responses to incidents on mental health units, including patients who are absent without leave. Police in England and Wales have specific powers under section 136 of the MHA. Section 136 of the MHA is a police power. It authorises any police officer to remove someone, who appears to be mentally disordered, from a public place to a 'place of safety'. A person who has been detained under section 136 of the MHA must be assessed with a view to admission under the MHA. A 'place of safety' is broadly defined but is usually a hospital accident and emergency department or a police cell. Many hospitals have established specialist s136 MHA suites. This is an emergency power and is generally used in circumstances where a person is thought to be putting themselves at immediate risk.

The Act states:

If a person appears to a constable to be suffering from mental disorder and to be in immediate need of care or control, the constable may, if he thinks it necessary to do so in the interests of that person or for the protection of other persons—

(a) remove the person to a place of safety within the meaning of section 135, or

(b) if the person is already at a place of safety within the meaning of that section, keep the person at that place or remove the person to another place of safety.

(1A) The power of a constable under subsection (1) may be exercised where the mentally disordered person is at any place, other than—

(a) any house, flat or room where that person, or any other person, is living, or

(b) any yard, garden, garage or outhouse that is used in connection with the house, flat or room, other than one that is also used in connection with one or more other houses, flats or rooms.

The use of section 136 of the MHA relies on the assessment of the individual police officers involved. There is no need for a formal medical diagnosis – recent changes to the use of section 136 are discussed in the next section. The purpose of section 136 is for a mental health assessment to be carried out by a psychiatrist and an AMHP. The period of detention lasts up to 24 hours. The MHA Code of Practice and locally agreed protocols emphasise that these assessments should be completed as quickly as possible.

The use of section 136 of the MHA

The monitoring of the use of section 136 has been generally poor. It is widely accepted that there has been an increase in its use over the past 20 years. As with other compulsory powers there are long-standing concerns that BAME groups, particularly young Black men, are overrepresented in section 136 detentions (Rogers and Faulkner, 1987; Dunn and Fahy, 1990; Bhui et al, 2003). This is a crucial issue as it means that in many cases, the first contact that a person has with mental health services is via the police or other areas of the CJS. It is, perhaps, not too surprising that section 136 MHA assessments are much more likely to take place outside of standard office hours. The demands on police in mental health work increase when normal support services are not more widely available. Borschmann et al (2010) indicate that the 'typical' section 136 patient is a young, single, working-class male with a past history of mental illness – a group which is much less likely than others in the population to access general health care including mental health services. Borschmann et al's study also noted that this group tended not to be registered with a GP. The Independent Police Complaints Commission (IPCC) carried out a major study of the use of section 136 in 2005/2006. In this study, 11,500 patients were assessed in custody and 5,900 in a mental health setting. The report highlighted significant variations between forces. Some of these can be explained by local conditions – for example Sussex police covers Beachy Head which is the site of a number of suicides. This study also confirmed Browne's (2009) finding that Black people were almost twice as likely as other groups to be subject to section 136.

Table 3.1: Decision points in the criminal justice system

Decision point	Factors to consider	Mental health legal and policy framework
Policing	All policing involves officers making judgements. People with mental health problems are citizens so come into contact with the police in a wide range of situations. The National Decision Making Model and the Code of Ethics provide the basis for police decisions. There are specific powers under the MHA and the PACE (College of Policing, nd).	• Section 136 MHA. • PACE. • Use of police cells for detention under section 136 of the MHA is limited. It has to be authorised by an inspector (or above). • Under-18s cannot be held in a police cell if they are detained under section 136 of the MHA. • 135 MHA warrants with AMHPs. • Detained patients who are missing or AWOL.
Supporting victims	MIND's (2015) *At risk yet dismissed* study found that people with mental health problems are: • three times more likely to be a victim of crime than the general population; • five times more likely to be a victim of assault (rising to 10 times more likely for women); • more likely to be a repeat victim and experience different types of crime; • far less likely to be satisfied with the service and support they receive (MIND, 2015).	Youth Justice and Criminal Evidence Act 1999 (YJCEA). • Special measures available at the court's discretion to enable the victim/witness to provide best evidence. • Screens to shield witnesses from the defendant. • Giving evidence via a live video. • Giving evidence in private. A 'vulnerable witness' includes: • all child/juvenile witnesses (anyone under 18). Any witness who might be vulnerable as they: • are suffering from a mental disorder (as defined by the Mental Health Act 1983); • experience a significant impairment of intelligence and social functioning; • or have a physical disability or are suffering from a physical disorder. Intimidated witnesses are defined by section 17 of the YJCEA as: • those suffering from fear or distress in relation to testifying in the case; • complainants in sexual offences are automatically (section 17(4)) regarded as intimated witness but they can opt out of these processes if they wish (CPS, nd).

(continued)

Table 3.1: Decision points in the criminal justice system (continued)

Decision point	Factors to consider	Mental health legal and policy framework
Police custody	Custody officers have a key role in the assessment of vulnerable people, who come into custody. The custody environment poses particular risks: • potential impact on individual mental health; • retraumatisation; • self-harm and suicide; • pressure leading to false statements or confessions.	PACE. Three groups considered additionally vulnerable in custody: • all juveniles (under 18s); • adults with a learning disability; • adults with a mental health problem. PACE created the role of the AA to 'facilitate the interview' and ensure that the detained person is aware of their rights, general welfare.
Prosecution	CPS makes decisions on prosecuting cases. The fact that someone has a mental illness should be *one* of the factors considered. Others might include: • the nature of the alleged offence; • wider public safety; • whether the individual is receiving treatment.	The CPS has to decide: • there is evidence to secure a conviction; • prosecution is in the public interest.
The courts	Research literature has identified the extent of mental health problems among prisoners. The courts have a range of powers to arrange a mental health assessment. These are, in fact, used comparatively rarely.	Court powers include: • Section 35 of the MHA (1983): admission to hospital for an assessment. It initially lasts for up to 28 days. • Section 36 of the MHA (1983) can be used by the Crown Court to admit to hospital for treatment. In a very small number of cases, the issue arises as to whether the defendant is fit to plead. This issue is decided by the judge on the basis of two medical reports one of which must come from a section 12 MHA approved doctor.
Sentencing	The majority of cases where a person has a mental health problem are sentenced within the normal range of sentences open to the courts. There are a range of sentences open where mental health issues are identified. In these cases, judges will consider reports from psychiatrists before deciding on a sentence.	Sentencing options/considerations: • Mental state: considered in cases where defendants plead not guilty on the grounds of diminished responsibility. • Mental Health Treatment Requirement (MHTR) is available to the courts as a sentencing option for community orders.

Table 3.1: Decision points in the criminal justice system (continued)

Decision point	Factors to consider	Mental health legal and policy framework
		• Section 37 MHA – hospital order. The purpose of the order is to divert offenders to psychiatric care. • Section 41 – restriction order. This is imposed in section 37 cases where the court feels that it is 'necessary for the protection of the public from serious harm'. This group of patients are usually admitted to Secure Units or the Special Hospitals. These patients are subject to social supervision when they are discharged. They will also be under the local Multi Agency Public Protection Arrangements (MAPPA). • Section 45A – hybrid order: the offender returns to prison from hospital to complete their sentence when considered well enough to do so.
Post-sentencing	The WHO Trencin (2008) statement outlines the fundamental principle that: individuals should not be denied healthcare because of their status as prisoners. HM Inspectorate of Prisons for England and Wales provide independent scrutiny of the conditions for and treatment of prisoners and other detainees (HM Inspectorate of Prisons, nd).	Prison mental health: • All prisoners are assessed on reception. • Mental health in-reach teams have been established to identify and support those prisoners with the greatest mental health needs. • Acutely ill prisoners can be transferred to forensic mental health services under section 47 or section 48 of the MHA.
Partnership working	Police and Crime Commissioners – first elections 2012. PCCs are elected to ensure police were accountable to communities – replaces police authority system. They decide: • policing plans; • the police budget; • the amount of Council Tax charged for the police. Police forces will be key agencies in a range of partnerships with health, education and welfare service providers.	The Crime and Disorder Act (1998) made partnerships a statutory duty for the agencies. Multi Agency Safeguarding Hubs (MASH). Adult Safeguarding Boards. MAPPA panels manage the supervision of violent and sexual offenders.

Source: Adapted from Cummins, I. (2016) *Mental health and the criminal justice system: a social work perspective*. Northwich: Critical Publishing

The use of police cells as a place of safety

Police cells can be used as a 'place of safety'. This is a far from ideal intervention and cells should only be used in 'exceptional circumstances'. Police custody is a pressurised, busy and often chaotic environment. There is clearly the potential for this to have a negative impact on an individual's mental health. Police officers are called upon to manage very difficult situations such as self-harm or attempted suicide often with little training or support. The physical environment of a police cell also needs to be taken into account when considering the potential impact of custody. A cell is a bare concrete space with a mattress and a steel toilet. Hampson (2011) argues that in practice exceptional means that the patient is 'too disturbed to be managed elsewhere'. Her Majesty's Inspectorate of Constabulary's (HMIC) 2013 study, *A criminal use of police cells*, examined in detail 70 cases where a cell had been used as a place of safety. At the time of writing, it is estimated that 36 per cent of all section 136 detentions involve the use of police custody. There are significant variations between or even within forces. This is the result of different local service provision. The most common reason for a police cell being used was that the person was drunk and/or violent or had a history of violence

There is very limited research which examines service-user perspectives on the experience of being detained under section 136. As the HMIC (2013) review notes, the experience can be, if the individual is taken to police custody, akin to being arrested. In custody, they are treated in the same way as any other person. The booking-in process is the same – it would include being searched. On occasions, because of concerns about self-harm or suicide, clothing may be taken away from the detained person. There will almost certainly be periods of delay – in custody or an accident and emergency department. Jones and Mason's (2002) study highlighted that from a service-user perspective this is a custodial not a therapeutic experience. In this study, service users made clear that the routine of being booked into custody was a dehumanising one. They also felt that police officers were too quick to assess that they were at risk of self-harm, meaning that there was an increased risk that they would be placed in a paper suit. Riley et al (2011) confirm this dissatisfaction with the process. In particular, the participants in the study felt that they were being treated like criminals for experiencing distress. Some felt that their mental health had worsened because of their time in custody.

MS v UK

The case of *MS v UK* which was decided in the European Court of Human Rights (ECHR) in 2012, demonstrates illustrates the potential difficulties that can arise. MS was detained under section 136 of the MHA following an assault on a relative. When he was assessed at the police station, it was decided that he needed to be transferred to psychiatric care. There then followed a series of delays and arguments between mental health services as to which unit would be the most appropriate to meet MS's mental health needs. This argument went on for so long that the 72-hour limit of section 136 was passed. The limit has now been reduced to 24 hours. MS was still in police custody and this has a dramatic impact on his mental state. As a result of paranoid delusional ideas, he refused food. The ECHR held that the treatment of MS constituted a breach of article 3 which prohibits inhumane and degrading treatment. This is clearly an unusual case but it illustrates the potential issues that arise. The judgment made it clear that the initial decision to detain MS under mental health legislation was valid and justified.

The Health and Social Care Information (HSCIC) data shows that in the majority of cases those individuals assessed following the police use of section 136 were not formally admitted to hospital – that is, detained under section 2 or 3 of the MHA 1983. One of the major difficulties when examining the use of section 136 is the danger that there is too narrow a focus on outcomes. It is a fallacy to argue that section 136 has not been used appropriately if the person is not detained. The test of section 136 is whether the officer thinks 'that it is necessary to do so in the interests of that person or for the protection of others'. Police officers must respond to the emergency that they face; if mental health professionals carry out an assessment and alternatives to hospital are organised then that does not mean the police officer's decision was incorrect. The whole purpose of section 136 is for an assessment to be carried out, not for a formal admission to hospital. Borschmann et al's 2010 study is an analysis of the use of section 136 in a South London Trust. The analysis showed that 41.2 per cent of the cases did not lead to hospital admission, 34.4 per cent led to admission under the MHA and 23.1 per cent to an informal admission.

The use of section 136 of the MHA is a very important area. It raises very important civil liberty issues as well as wider ones about the treatment of people experiencing mental health problems. As Latham (1997) points out, it allows for an individual without any formal mental health training or qualifications to detain someone. There is no appeal mechanism. Unlike emergency detentions under sections 5(2) and 5(4) of the MHA the person with the power has no medical training and no medical evidence is required for the power to be enacted. In fact, the purpose of detention under section 136 is for psychiatric assessment. However, it is important to bear in mind that this is just one area of mental health work in which police officers are potentially involved. There is a danger that debates about the working of section 136 overshadow the whole debate in this field.

The reform of section 136 of the Mental Health Act

Ongoing concerns about section 136 of the MHA led to a review in 2014. In 2017, significant changes to section 136 were introduced.

- *Length of the section*: under the original legislation a person could be held under section 136 for *up to 72 hours*. Local arrangements and protocols were in place to try and ensure that no individual was detained under section 136 of the MHA for such a long period. However, it was not unheard of – particularly if there were delays in finding a hospital bed when it was decided an individual should be admitted to hospital. The reduction to 24 hours meant that legislation in England and Wales was brought into line with similar powers in Scotland.
- *Duty to consult*: the duty to consult was introduced to support and improve police decision making in mental health emergency situations. Before using the section 136 powers, a police officer is now required by new section 136(1C) to consult a specified health professional. The consultation allows a police officer to receive relevant mental health information and advice. This will assist them to decide the course of action that is in the best interests of the person concerned. If it is not practicable to consult, for example, because delays may place an individual or other members of the community at risk, then the police officer can still use section 136 powers. The changes do not specifically outline what form the consultation should take. The consultation and how it will affect officer decisions will vary depending on the individual circumstances of each case. Factors that will have an impact here include whether the person has had previous contact with mental health services and records are available and whether the health professional is physically present. The duty to consult is an attempt to assist police officers. It does not remove their professional autonomy. At the time of writing, there is little research that has examined how the frequency of consultation or the overall impact of the duty.
- *Use of police cells as a place of safety*: this has been an area that has been the cause of ongoing concern. The use of police cells as places of safety had been decreasing. A police cell is widely recognised as a totally inappropriate environment for a person who is experiencing any form of acute mental distress (HMIC, 2013). The changes to legislation make the detention of a juvenile in a police cell under section 136 of the MHA unlawful in any circumstances.
- *The use of police stations as a place of safety*: a police station can now only be used as a place of safety for adults if:
  * the behaviour of the person poses an imminent risk of serious injury or death to themselves or another person;

- because of that risk, no other place of safety in the relevant police area can reasonably be expected to detain them; and
- so far as reasonably practicable, a healthcare professional will be present at the police station and available to them.

An officer of at least the rank of inspector must authorise the use of a police station in such circumstances (The Mental Health Act 1983 (Places of Safety Regulations 2017)).

Vulnerable adults in police custody

PACE (2004) provided key safeguards for the protection of vulnerable adults – that is, adults with mental health problems or learning disabilities – while in police custody. Along with the standard procedures and rights such as the provision of legal advice and the taping of interviews, such individuals have to be interviewed with an appropriate adult present. Custody sergeants have a key role to play in this process as they, in effect, carry out a risk assessment of every individual who comes into custody. This section outlines the legal requirements of PACE (2004) in respect of adults with mental health problems. It will also examine the operation of these safeguards.

Police and Criminal Evidence Act and the role of the appropriate adult

Maxwell Confait was murdered in 1972. His body was found in his London bedsit. He had been strangled and the property set on fire. The case has never been solved. It would have profound implications for the wider administration of justice in England and Wales. In November 1972, three youths were convicted of arson with intent to endanger life. One was also found guilty of manslaughter and one was convicted of murder. The prosecution was based on confession evidence (Fisher, 1977). An initial appeal was rejected in July 1973. In June 1975, the cases were referred to the Court of Appeal. In October that year, the convictions were quashed. The appeals were followed by the establishment of a Royal Commission that reported in 1981. The changes that the Commission recommended were incorporated into PACE (1984). The investigation into the murder of Maxwell Confait took place in a very different cultural and legal climate to the one that now exists. This is clearly not a defence of the treatment of the three youths or to minimise the devastating impact that it had on them or their families. The CJS had yet to experience the shocks caused by a series of miscarriages of justice such as the wrongful conviction of the Birmingham Six.

The role of the appropriate adult

The introduction of PACE led to wider protections for those being interviewed by the police. The new framework included the tape recording of interviews. Three groups – juveniles, adults with learning difficulties and adults with mental health problems –were afforded additional protections. There have been miscarriages of justice since, often involving vulnerable adults. It is important to recognise that PACE reforms are the direct result of a miscarriage of justice. While offering additional protections to vulnerable adults, PACE can only be one feature of a wider system.

The role of the appropriate adult (AA) was introduced to ensure that vulnerable individuals were afforded additional protections while in police custody. The AA does not enjoy legal privilege in the way that a solicitor does. The AA role is something of a hybrid. The AA is not an advocate, though the AA might take on this function in certain circumstances. The AA will be concerned to ensure that the interview is carried out fairly and that any welfare needs that the detained person has are addressed. For example, the AA should ensure that there are regular breaks in interviewing and so on.

The AA has a key role to ensure that detained persons are aware of their rights in custody under Code C (para 31). In most scenarios, the detained person will be in custody and then an AA will be called for. When the AA arrives at the station they will have to introduce themselves to the detained person and clearly explain their role. As we have seen there are some ambiguities in the AA role. It is important that the detained person recognises that the AA is not a representative or able to advise on legal matters. If the detained person is not legally represented or has waived the right to be so, the AA can decide not to proceed with the interview until representation has been arranged. There are some arguments that would see such an intervention as paternalistic and overriding the wishes of an individual. As a social worker, I acted as an AA on numerous occasions, and I cannot think of a single case where a detained person did not want legal representation. If this situation has arisen, I think that I would have definitely overridden the detained person's wishes and arranged for legal representation.

The key roles of the appropriate adult

- Ensure the detained person is aware of their rights (Code C, para 31).
- Ensure the interview is conducted properly and fairly and is not 'oppressive' (Code C, para 11.16).
- Make representations at any review of detention or other procedures such as fingerprinting (Code D, paras 1.11–14).

The role of the AA has been a feature of the CJS since the reforms of the early 1980s. However, there are still barriers to full implementation. It might be unrealistic to hope that all vulnerable adults would be interviewed with an AA present. The lack of training that police officers receive, the poor sharing of information across services and the inherent difficulties in making an assessment of any individual's mental state within pressured custody are the key barriers (Cummins, 2007). Despite progress in these areas, these barriers have not been eliminated.

The framers of PACE envisaged that the role of the AA would be undertaken in adult cases by a professional – social worker or nurse – with a knowledge of mental health and/or learning disabilities. From its introduction, PACE allowed for others to undertake the role – apart from the defence solicitor or a co-accused essentially anyone over the age of 18 can take on the role. In a number of areas, there are volunteer schemes to cover the provision of AAs. In Medford et al (2003), there is an example of a doorman from a hotel next to the police station taking on the role. This is an extreme and isolated example. Of course, the individual may have carried out the role in exemplary fashion. However, it highlights a fundamental weakness and contradiction in the role. If this is a key role protecting vulnerable people in the CJS, it cannot be exercised in such a haphazard fashion. Bartlett and Sandland (2003) have argued that there is confusion at the heart of the role that the AA is asked to play. This confusion stems from the ambiguity of such terms as 'facilitate communication' and 'fair interview'. The role cuts across the welfare and justice axis.

The law in this area has stemmed from cases where the question at issue was the suitability of the individual acting as an AA. Pierpoint (2000) has highlighted the way that a parent taking on the role can possibly undermine the position of detained juveniles. Such an argument could be similarly deployed in cases of adults being questioned when the AA is a family member or has a close relationship with the individual in custody. This is supported by the decision in *DPP v Blake* where an estranged father was not seen to be neutral. In *R v Morse*, it was held that a father should not have taken on the role as his low IQ meant that he was unable to understand the scope and nature of the role. In *R v Cox* the confession evidence of a woman was held to be admissible despite the fact that her mother, who acted as the AA, had learning difficulties and mental health problems. There is a lack of clarity in legislation and practice here. The protections of PACE should apply if the custody sargeant has reason to believe that the detained person has a mental health problem. This is not, of course, the same as being acutely unwell. The fluid and changing nature of mental health problems does not mean they are all necessary relevant to these sorts of decisions.

In an era when the state is seeking to and has reduced the rights of suspects, it is worth asking why and how the role of the AA came about. It was part of a series of measures to protect vulnerable individuals from abuse within the criminal justice process, particularly the danger of self-incrimination. The evidence from a series of cases is that the need for those protections still exists. As Haley and Swift (1988) suggest, the overarching aim is for the courts to hear more reliable evidence. It is in interests of all citizens to support such moves.

Adults with mental health problems or a learning disability are much more likely to be victims of crime, particularly and increasingly hate crime, than perpetrators. PACE offers additional protections to vulnerable adults if they are in police custody. One of the difficulties with PACE is that the decision as to whether an appropriate adult is required is one that is made by custody sergeants. I should emphasise that I am not being critical of custody sergeants here or suggesting that they ignore the mental health needs of vulnerable adults. I am highlighting that custody sergeants are asked to take these decisions, often with little further information. The custody environment makes these decisions even more difficult. Custody sergeants are experienced police officers not mental health nurses. Mental health problems can be difficult to assess. The custody environment is a pressurised and stressful one, which is bound to impact on individual behaviour. The assessment of an individual's mental health can be made more complicated by the influence of drugs and alcohol. The overall impact is that relatively few adults in police custody are interviewed with an AA present.

Gaps in the operation of PACE safeguards

There to help (National Appropriate Adult Network [NAAN], 2015) highlighted the gaps in operation of the PACE safeguards. Police forces continue to struggle to find professionals or volunteers who will attend as AA. The report also highlighted that there were ongoing difficulties in assessing vulnerable adults and ensuring that they were properly supported while in custody. These failings are the result of systemic failing. *There to help 2* was published in 2019 (NAAN, 2019). NAAN approached 43 police forces as well as the British Transport Police for information about the support provided to vulnerable adults in police custody. Thirty-nine forces replied and 31 forces were able to provide data. There was only one force where this information was not recorded. The report indicated that a need had been identified and recorded in 5.9 per cent of cases of detentions in 2017/2018. This represented a significant increase from the 2013/2014 figure, which was 3.1 per cent. These figures need to be placed in a wider context of the experience of mental illness and learning disability in the population. However, research suggests (NAAN, 2009) that between 11 and 22 per cent of adults detained in police custody are vulnerable under the terms outlined in PACE (2004). These figures indicate that possibly as many as three-quarters of vulnerable adults in custody are not being identified as such by current processes. This means that a significant group of vulnerable adults do not receive the additional protections that PACE (2004) provides. It is perhaps not surprising that there are significant variations between forces of the number of interviews with an AA present – 0.2–15.7 per cent for interviews in custody. This is explained by the variation in local AA schemes and other demographic factors.

One of the most positive findings from NAAN (2019) is that there has been a significant increase in organised provision of AA services. Of 174 local authorities, 143 (83 per cent) have an AA scheme for adults. This represents an increase from 53 per cent recorded in *There to help*. Of the schemes, 45 per cent provided cover 24 hours a day, seven days a week. In many areas there are still significant gaps in service provision. Police custody is an environment that potentially places vulnerable people at increased risk. The longer one spends in that environment, the greater the potential risk. The report concludes that in 2017/2018 at least 111,445 detentions and voluntary interviews of vulnerable adults took place without an AA present.

It is now nearly 40 years since the introduction of PACE (1984). There are still significant gaps in the provision of AA schemes across England and Wales. This is an area where there are concerns about the risks involved. These risks include the impact on the vulnerable adult such as a deterioration in their mental health or possible self-harm and suicide. Alongside these risks, there are others such as the potential impact of a false confession. *There to help 2* recommends that a fundamental change is required to address these issues. As it stands, there is no statutory duty on local authorities to ensure that independent AA provision exists. This is contrasted with the situation with children. The Crime and Disorder Act (1998) created a duty on local authorities to provide such services for children. It is difficult to see, apart from perhaps cost, what the arguments would/might be against extending the duty to vulnerable adults.

Deaths in police custody

Advice on ensuring the safety of those with mental health problems forms part of *Guidance on the safer detention and handling of persons in police custody* (Association of Chief Police Officers and the Home Office, 2006). The guidance itself is not comprehensive. In any event, for it to be followed successfully, it is dependent on police officers making appropriate assessments of an individual's mental state and any potential risks. The custody setting is a largely neglected area of study. Skinns (2011), following the work of Choongh (1997) and Newburn and Hayman (2002), explores the way that the police fundamentally shape the nature of the custody environment. Despite an increasing range of other agencies and professionals – social workers, doctors, lawyers, drug workers, lay visitors and AAs – having a role in the custody process, this remains the case. The custody process is part of the police investigation and prosecution of crime. Choongh (1997) suggests that for a small number of suspects who have regular contacts with the police, custody is used as a mechanism to impose discipline and establish authority.

Deaths in police custody are deaths that might be the result of traumatic injuries or a lack of proper care (Gannoni and Bricknell, 2019). PACE (2004) allows for detention in custody in most cases for up to 24 hours. By the end of that period, a detained person must be charged, bailed or a decision reached that no further action will be taken. Detention before charge is reviewed after six hours and then after nine hours. The review must be conducted by an officer of at least the rank of inspector who has not been directly involved in the investigation. The average detention in police custody lasts around six hours (Dehaghani, 2016). The police can apply to hold an individual for up to 36 or 96 hours if they are suspected of a serious crime, such as murder. A person arrested under the Terrorism Act can be held without charge for up to 14 days. The police can release a person on conditional bail if they have been charged and they have grounds to think that they may:

- commit another offence;
- fail to turn up at court;
- intimidate other witnesses; and
- obstruct the course of justice.

Conditions might include address or other restrictions of freedom – not to approach other individuals or the imposition of a curfew.

Custody is a situation that contains a number of risks. These are potentially increased when an individual has mental health problems. The assessment process that custody officers carry out is a challenging one. It requires a range of skills, not the least of which is the ability to work in a highly pressurised environment. There appear to be a number of variables that may be affecting the decision-making process. These will include:

- skills, training, experience and attitudes towards mental illness of the arresting officers and the custody sergeant;
- local systems that have been established;
- nature of the offence;
- circumstances of the arrest and the presentation of the individual who has been arrested; and
- environmental factors such as the other pressures in the custody suite and on the officer at the time.

The role of the custody sergeant is one that is under-researched. This is surprising given the pivotal role that they have and the level of responsibility that is placed upon them. One of the impacts of reality TV programmes such as *24 Hours in Police Custody* is that the wider public are more aware of the role and the demands that it places on individual officers. Cummins (2006) interviewed custody sergeants about their work. One of the recurring theme in these interviews was that the officers felt a very strong duty of care is owed to those in custody. This was held to be ultimately the responsibility of the sergeant on duty. In the study, the officers felt that they were unlikely to receive meaningful support from senior managers in the event of a death or other serious incident in custody. The prospect of the devastating personal and professional effects of a death in custody loomed large in the working lives of these officers. The result was that officers relied on their professional experience or, on occasions, previous knowledge of individuals in custody in order to carry out assessments.

One of the difficulties that custody officers potentially face is the lack of information about an individual in custody. The provision of specialist support in custody has made improvements in this area. The reduction in the use of police cells for detention under section 136 of the MHA is one of the key developments. These changes come after other changes such as regular checks on detainees and the removal of potential ligature points from cells (Baker, 2016; Payne-James, 2016). These are, of course, all welcome but police custody will never be a therapeutic environment. In addition to the fact that an individual has been arrested, environmental factors such as lack of privacy and poor hygiene in cells serve to heighten feelings of vulnerability (Payne-James, 2016). To these factors, it is important to add the potential retraumatising impact of processes such as intimate personal searching. Alongside potential mental health risks, it is important that physical health factors such as the impact of alcohol and substance misuse or being assaulted in a violent altercation are not overlooked (Payne-James, 2016).

In 2018/2019 the Independent Office for Police Conduct (IOPC) recorded a total of 16 deaths in police custody. Ten of the people who died had experienced mental health problems (INQUEST, 2019). Article 2 of the ECHR requires an inquest and inquiry into deaths in police custody (Baker, 2016; Russell, 2017). In the UK, deaths in police custody are investigated through the coronial system and the IOPC (Angiolini, 2017; Her Majesty's Inspectorate of Constabulary and Fire and Rescue Services, 2017).

The IOPC produces an annual report that examines *deaths in or following police custody*. These cases involve deaths that happen while a person is being arrested or taken into detention and the deaths of people who have been arrested or have been detained by police under the MHA (1983). These cases are a broad category and may have taken place on police or private premises, in a public place or in a police vehicle.

The IOPC report covers deaths that happen:

- during or following police custody where injuries that contributed to the death happened during the period of detention;
- in or on the way to hospital (or other medical premises) during or following transfer from scene of arrest or police custody;
- as a result of injuries or other medical problems that are identified or that develop while a person is in custody; and
- while a person is in police custody having been detained under section 136 of the MHA (1983) or other related legislation.

The IOPC figures do not include:

- suicides that occur after a person has been released from police custody; and
- deaths that happen where the police are called to help medical staff to restrain people who are not under arrest.

The IOPC also examines:

- apparent suicides following police custody.

This is defined as apparent suicides that happen within two days of release from police custody. The IPOC will also examine apparent suicides that take place more than two days after release from custody, if the time spent in custody may be relevant to the death (IOPC, nd).

Conclusion

Webb (2006) notes that despite the great social and economic progress that has been made, society seems more concerned than ever with risk. There is an obsession with risk which includes a hankering for a risk-free world or zero risk. For Beck (1992) this is a developmental phase of modernity as the social, political, economic and individual risk become disconnected from the institutions that are established to monitor and protect. Policing alongside other public services are inevitably caught up in these developments. Webb (2006) outlines the spiralling effect where publics feel that governments and their agencies should anticipate and eliminate risk. When the inevitable systems failures occur then this leads to increased demands for action or new modes of audit and regulation. Policing increasingly involves working with vulnerable people in conditions of uncertainty. The role of the custody officer is an example.

The custody setting and the decision making of police officers is a key area. It is neglected in the literature relating to mentally disordered offenders. In particular, the experiences of custody sergeants carrying out the role have not been explored in depth. The focus of research in this area of mental illness and the CJS has concentrated on prisons or the courts with an emphasis on measuring the extent on mental illness among offenders. Singleton et al's (1998) study remains the key analysis of the extent of mental health problems among the prison population. The Corston Inquiry (2008) was established to examine the experiences of women in prison in a broad perspective but there is a clear focus on mental health issues. Steel et al (2007) examined the effectiveness of prison mental health in-reach teams. The Bradley Review (2009) considered the impact of mental health issues across the CJS. Dyer (2013) examined the effectiveness of liaison and diversion schemes that seek to prevent people with mental health problems being sent to prison. Previous research on policing and mental illness has focused on beat officers (Teplin, 1984) and/or their assessment of individuals experiencing acute mental distress (Jones and Mason, 2002).

The recent retrenchment in mental health and wider public services mean that the police face increasing demands in this area (Edmondson and Cummins, 2014). Police involvement in mental health work has to be viewed as part of their role in wider community safety and the protection of vulnerable people. As this work shows, these challenges are both individual and organisational.

Further reading

Bartkowiak-Théron, I. and Asquith, N.L. (2016) Conceptual divides and practice synergies in law enforcement and public health: some lessons from policing vulnerability in Australia. *Policing & Society*, 27(3), 276–288.

Borschmann, R.D., Gillard, S., Turner, K., Chambers, M. and O'Brien, A. (2010) Section 136 of the Mental Health Act: a new literature review. *Medicine, Science and the Law*, 50(1), 34–39.

Bradley, K. (2009) *The Bradley report: Lord Bradley's review of people with mental health problems or learning disabilities in the criminal justice system*. London: DH.

Browne, D. (2009) Black communities, mental health and the criminal justice system. In J. Reynolds, R. Muston, T. Heller et al. (eds) *Mental health still matters*. Basingstoke: Palgrave Macmillan.

Corston, J. (Chair) (2008) *A report by Baroness Jean Corston of a review of women with particular vulnerabilities in the Criminal Justice system*. Available at: https://webarchive.nationalarchives.gov.uk/20130206102659/http:/www.justice.gov.uk/publications/docs/corston-report-march-2007.pdf

Department of Health (1998) *Modernising mental health services safe, sound and supportive health services*. London: HMSO.

Department of Health (2014) *Mental health crisis care concordat: improving outcomes for people experiencing mental health crisis*. London: Department of Health.

Durcan, G., Saunders, A., Gadsby, B. and Hazard, A. (2014) *The Bradley report five years on: an independent review of progress to date and priorities for further development.* Centre for Mental Health. Available at: http://www.centreformentalhealth.org.uk/the-bradley-report-five-years-on

4

'Street-level psychiatrists'?

Introduction

The title of this chapter comes from Lipsky's (1980) classic study, *Street level bureaucracy*. Lipsky's work is the study of the impact of financial crisis on welfare services in New York. It was also a period when the impact of the first wave of deinstitutionalisation was being felt (Cummins, 2020d). This led to an increase in homelessness but also more frequent contact between the police and people experiencing mental health problems. 'Street-level psychiatrist' was a term that officers used in interviews with Lipsky to sum up the new role that they felt they were being forced to play. The term was used in a sardonic fashion, not to claim any great expertise. The opposite is the case as officers were highlighting their lack of training and knowledge in this area. This chapter examines mental health work in the context of broader 'cop culture' before outlining new models of policing such as street triage that have been developed.

Police decision making

The Association of Chief Police Officers (ACPO) developed the National Decision Making (NDM) model (ACPO, 2012) to inform all officers in the complex policing decisions they are required to make on a daily basis. At the centre of the model, the police values and mission statement commits the police to 'act with integrity, compassion, courtesy and patience, showing neither fear nor favour in what we do. We will be sensitive to the needs and dignity of victims and demonstrate respect for the human rights of all' (ACPO, 2012: 3).

Officers are required to keep these principles at the centre of decision making. The NDM model is applicable to all police work and appears particularly relevant to the context of police work where mental health issues are present. Figure 4.1 illustrates the model.

This approach requires officers to assess the situation while taking account of what powers, if any, they have to act. For example, in mental health work are they the most appropriate professionals to intervene? As we have seen, one of the frustrations of police officers is that they feel that they are often not the most appropriate professionals but they are the only ones available or are the first to respond in a crisis or emergency.

Figure 4.1: Police national decision making

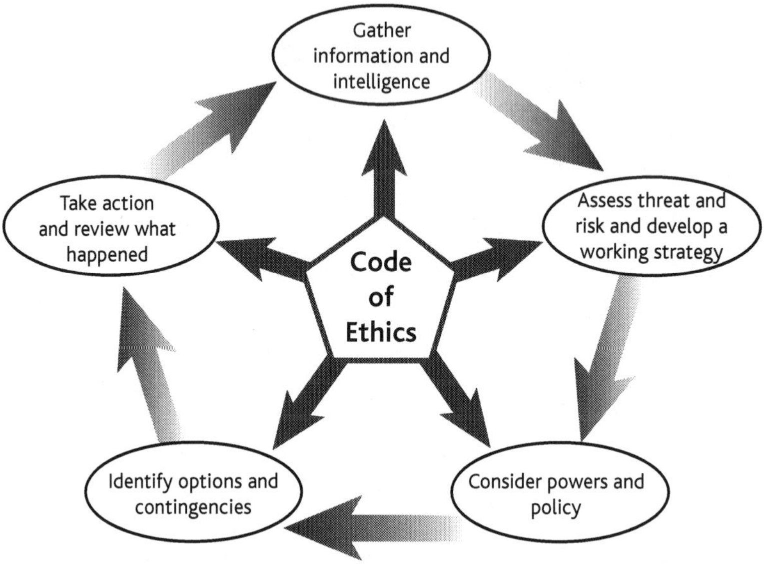

Source: College of Policing (nd). Contains information licensed under the non-commercial College licence https://www.app.college.police.uk/app-content/national-decision-model/the-national-decision-model/#the-model.

In October 2018, the House of Commons Home Affairs Committee published a report, *Policing for the future*. Dee Collins, Chief Constable of West Yorkshire Police, in giving evidence stated that '83% of my time in terms of delivering services is not about crime'. In situating this work in the wider context of modern policing, the inquiry highlighted that:

> A prominent theme emerging throughout this inquiry was the increasing volume of police work arising from identifying and managing various forms of vulnerability, including safeguarding vulnerable adults who cross their path, being first-on-scene during a mental health crisis, undertaking child protection work on a multi-agency basis, and dealing with repeat missing person incidents, including looked-after children.

Despite the difficulties with the collection of accurate and robust data, including the question of how to define what should be regarded as a 'mental health incident', the broad overall trend is clear. Police officers are increasingly involved in mental health work, either responding to individuals in crisis or working alongside other agencies.

There have always been overlaps between models of law enforcement and public health. Police officers can have a key role to play in situations in which individuals are experiencing some sort of crisis related to mental health problems. The Sainsbury Centre for Mental Health's (2008) study suggested that up to 15 per cent of incidents dealt with by the police include some sort of mental health issue or concern. It also calls for the exercise of a range of skills. In his 2013 report, Lord Adebowale described mental health work as 'core police business'. The police have considerable discretion in terms of their response. They may well be the emergency service that is first contacted by the relatives of those in acute distress, who are, for example, putting themselves or others at risk. If a person is acutely distressed in a public place then the likelihood of some form of police involvement is increased significantly. There have been increasing concerns about the demands that mental health work places on police time and resources. In addition, police officers feel that they are ill-equipped to deal with mental health crises. Responding to people in mental health crisis has become one of the most important concerns for frontline officers.

Police organisational culture and mental health work

In the recent debates about the role of the police in mental health work, there are ongoing arguments as to whether police officers should be involved in the field at all. Alongside this, there is a view that mental health work does not fit easily into what can be termed 'cop culture'. This is a rather loose and flexible term. However, it is used here to represent the core notions that see policing as dynamic, responsive, action–driven and problem–solving. It is argued that mental health work does not fit neatly with these notions. There are rarely immediate satisfactory solutions to crisis or other situations. Of course, it is not a crime to be mentally ill. Many police officers argue that it is not therefore their role to become involved in this area of work. Service-users and mental health professionals are concerned that the involvement of the police is not only stigmatising, it may well place individuals at risk.

Using Bourdieu to analyse mental health services and policies

Bourdieu's conceptual framework of *field, habitus and capital* provides a set of tools that we can use to analyse the development of policies in the mental health and CJS spheres. Bourdieu (1998) defines a field as a 'structured social space, a field of forces'. This is a way of looking at the factors and individuals that influence the development of policy within a given area – the field. If we think of policing and mental health as a field, we can then think of the agencies, individuals and other groups that are actors or players in this field. These would include political figures such as the Secretary of State for Health and Social Care, influential celebrities who lead anti-stigma campaigns or raise awareness, the leaders of professional bodies, the National

Police Chiefs Council mental health lead, service-user groups and think tanks that influence policy such as the Sainsbury Centre. One advantage of this approach is that it avoids seeing policy as top-down and recognises that it is a dynamic process. The influence of particular individuals or agencies can increase depending on the circumstances. For example, the journalist Marjorie Wallace, the founder of Schizophrenia: A National Emergency (SANE) became increasingly influential during the community care crisis of the early 1990s (Cummins, 2020a). Wallace argued that community care reforms had put vulnerable people at risk. In addition, she argued that liberal professionals, in focusing on the rights of patients, marginalised and ignored carers and families. She went further, arguing that there needed to be reforms to the MHA that would allow for community treatment. This became part of a powerful and widely accepted critique of wider mental health policy. The reform of the MHA in 2007 saw the introduction of CTOs. In this field, the work of Inspector Michael Brown (OBE) is another great example. His *MentalHealthCop* blog (Brown, nd) and *@MentalHealthCop* twitter offered serving officers invaluable practical and sometimes legal advice on any issues relating to mental health and policing. He became an influential and important figure within this field – being asked to give evidence to the Home Affairs Select Committee but also making regular media appearances.

Bourdieu use of the notion of field encourages us to examine the fluctuating and dynamic role of major actors. As in sport, the position on the field – we might see this as the actor's relative influence – changes frequently. Garrett (2007) argues that a field has three key elements within it. The first is the impact that it has on the development of the *habitus* of individuals within it. Habitus is a key term for Bourdieu. Habitus is 'the way society becomes deposited in persons in the form of lasting dispositions, or trained capacities and structured propensities to think, feel and act in determinant ways, which then guide them' (Wacquant, 2005: 316).

If we apply this is in the area of policing, we can see that officers develop a professional habitus – this is true of all professions. It is important to recognise that Bourdieu does not see individuals as automatons who act in totally predictable ways. However, he argues that individuals develop a set of ways of looking at the world and reacting to it. Professionals in their training, but also in the way that they are socialised into the profession, develop a set of approaches and values. These then help to inform the way that they behave and respond to situations or problems.

Garrett (2007) argues that a field seeks to maintain its own autonomy. The actors within any given field are in some form of competition with each other. The result is the constant ebbing and flowing of policies and approaches. Using the notion of field allows for these policies to be seen not as contradictory but as competing elements of a strategic battle. The notion of field encourages us to examine the influences on the development of policy in nuanced fashion. The interaction between the notions of field and habitus is crucial. Wacquant (1998) argues that in themselves they do not have the 'capacity to determine social action'. It is the interplay between the two that needs to be considered. Even if we assume that there is agreement across a field, it does not mean that all individuals in a given position within that field will act in the same way. Field has a key role to play in the development of the habitus of any individual located there.

Habitus is thus a product of, but also a contributing factor to, the development of an organisational working culture. This is as true for the police as any other organisation. There are distinctive features in policing. It is a command and control organisation with a clear hierarchical structure. Reiner's (1992b) outline of 'cop culture' has been very influential in setting and shaping debates about the nature of policing. He identified key elements of the police organisational culture. These included that it was essentially conservative. Reiner suggested that officers held a cynical and pessimistic view of the world. For Reiner, police officers are action orientated. Status is obtained by being a 'thief taker'. The working culture that is described here is also one that is politically conservative and on occasions racist, misogynistic and homophobic. Reiner highlighted the importance of loyalty both to fellow officers and the wider 'police family'. This is potentially a very positive aspect of police culture. However, it can also create insularity and hostility and place loyalty to the organisation above wider civic and professional values (Campeau, 2015). Officers see themselves as part of a 'thin blue line' that protects the community from criminal elements (Westmarland and Rowe, 2016). The idea of protecting the community is a key motivating factor for many recruits. Within such a cultural framework, there is the potential for mental health work to be seen as 'not proper policing' and thus having a lower status and organisational priority.

There is a danger in presenting police culture in monolithic terms as a reactionary or negative. Policing is no different to any other profession in having distinctive elements in its organisational culture. These elements attract some potential recruits but repel others. 'Organisational culture' is a very broad term (Denison, 1996). It is made up of a wide range of elements. These would include resources, policies and environmental factors that impact on the individual worker. The danger is that organisational culture is used as a tool to explain individual behaviour rather than one factor in shaping it (Martin, 2002). This is where the use of Bourdieu's analytical toolbox allows for a more nuanced understanding of the factors that shape individual decision making. Organisational culture is a neutral term but is generally used in a pejorative sense when policing is being discussed (Foster, 2003). In policing studies, there is a danger that Reiner's work – clearly vitally important – is given too much analytical power. Waddington (1999) argued that the 'canteen culture' that Reiner was outlining was an oral culture. It was full of bravado and dark humour which were essential defence mechanisms for officers who were dealing with crisis situations and examples of the worst aspects of human behaviour on a daily basis. This is a culture that one can see in other areas, for example, the military. It has been increasingly challenged. However, it remains powerful. Reuss-Ianni and Ianni (1999) argued that there are multiple cultures within policing – it is wrong to think of a force as a monolithic organisation. The nature of the organisation means that are clear differences between management approaches and the officers who are exercising their roles on the street. Alongside these internal differences, there are significant differences between the communities that police officers serve. These mean that the demands on those forces and the resultant organisational cultures will vary significantly across and within forces.

Reiner's original outline of 'cop culture' is now over 25 years old. This raises a question as to its current validity as a starting point for the analysis of police work and structure. The recruitment and working practices of the police have changed significantly since Reiner's work first appeared. These changes can be divided into two very broad areas. The first might be termed the police response to the equality and diversity agenda. The second area is the new modes of working with a range of agencies and partnership working. Such changes require new approaches but also a new set of skills – interagency working, empathy and problem solving.

Community policing

Community policing, rather than a reactive model, requires the police to work with local communities and relevant health and social welfare agencies to gain an insight into local problems (Skogan, 2008). These are not necessarily crime but they will involve a police response. As it stands, mental health is a prime example of these issues. This approach requires an organisational shift. There is a recognition that policing is often more concerned with the welfare of vulnerable people than the detection and arrest of offenders. On an organisational level, it means that police representatives are more involved in interagency and community forums. These moves have their roots in the 1980s. Holdaway (1986) outlines that such local partnerships were met with scepticism – with the police regarding them as 'talking shops'. There has been huge progress in overcoming the clash of organisational cultures that created barriers to partnership working. There was an inevitable clash between the command and control nature of the police and the statutory and voluntary organisations who were also represented on these working groups (O'Neill and McCarthy, 2014). The Crime and Disorder Act (1998) made involvement in such partnerships a statutory duty for the agencies. This was followed by the development of Local Neighbourhood Policing from 2008 onwards.

'Cop culture' can be read as a form of 'hegemonic masculinity' (Hearn, 2004). There have been clearly hugely significant changes that have taken place in society over the past 30 years since Reiner developed the concept. Profound changes in social and other attitudes in the areas of race, gender and sexuality are key here. For example, police forces being officially represented at Gay Pride marches would have been impossible in the 1980s. Loftus (2009) examines what she terms the 'politicisation of diversity'. The Macpherson Report (1999) outlined historical failings and abuse in the policing of BAME communities. Burke's (1994) research demonstrated that the discrimination and homophobia that gay and lesbian police officers faced reflected the response that these groups faced from the police. HMIC's (1999) report concluded that forces were failing to provide an adequate service to gay and lesbian citizens. There have been a range of initiatives aimed at the recruitment, retention and promotion of officers from minority communities and groups. These initiatives include the establishment of groups such as the Lesbian and Gay Police Association to support officers. The fact that these initiatives have been adopted at managerial levels does not necessarily mean that they have been smoothly adopted across policing. While acknowledging progress, it is important to recognise this history but also the work that still needs to be done.

Loftus (2010) revisited the classic Reiner notion of police culture. She identified a tension between the changes in the policy landscape such as the range of diversity initiatives and the continued existence of the characteristics that Reiner observed. Loftus (2010) highlighted that one of the strongest continuing factors was the 'them and us'/'the thin blue line' trope. There were two aspects to this. Rank and file officers saw themselves apart or often at odds with the senior management but also with the general public. Loftus did not hear the openly racist comments that Holdaway (1983) reported in his classic study of policing. However, Loftus noted derogatory comments aimed at young working class or marginalised communities. The notion of the 'police family' remained very powerful. Brough et al (2016) noted the strength of a strongly masculine police culture despite the changes to recruitment and other initiatives. However, Loftus identified some significant cultural changes. The first was the reduction in the social rituals – particularly those linked to drinking. Loftus (2010) identified that the 'job' was no longer seen as the key aspect of officers' lives. Policing was, like other public services, dominated by a culture of risk and risk management. Loftus (2010) concluded that despite these changes aspects of 'cop culture' clearly remain. This is because the fundamentals of policing remain – engaging with often powerless or vulnerable people in difficult, tense and demanding situations.

Kringen (2014: 368) argues that 'Feminist critiques illustrate that androcentric research fails to consider the impact of gender on crime and criminal justice'. Her systematic review of literature published in the field of women and policing between 1972 and 2012 concluded that there were three major domains: job performance; job experience; and blocked opportunities. Kringen (2014) also noted that the majority of research in this area is published in specialist journals. The knowledge generated thus remained at the margins of mainstream criminology. There is an ongoing concern that policing research is dominated by what we know about the experiences of male officers.

At its root, the diversity reform agenda has sought to remove the worst aspects of Reiner's *cop culture* (McLaughlin, 2007). The police are not the only profession that has gone on this journey. These reforms, though currently under challenge, have been seen as vital to the creation of a modern organisational work culture. Developments such as the Equality Act have given further protections to individuals and placed further responsibilities on employers. Alongside these policy changes, there has been a recognition of the benefits that diversity can bring – for example by recruiting from a broader base you bring new qualities to an organisation but also the police can serve communities more effectively. It would be naïve to assume that these changes mean that progress has been completely smooth or supported at all times. At the time of writing, the Equalities Minister Liz Truss has attacked the fundamentals that underpin the diversity and reform agenda in her speech 'The new fight for fairness' (Truss, 2020).

At its core, policing has a broader welfare function alongside the arrest and detention of offenders. In the final chapter, I explore in more depth the recent calls to 'defund the police'. One of the strongest arguments put forward by those such as Vitale (2017) is that the police are ill-equipped to carry out the wider welfare role. This is a result of what Vitale terms the 'warrior mentality'. Vitale suggests that police officers are being asked to intervene because of the wider retrenchment of social and welfare services. This is a view that many police officers might support. These issues are examined in depth in the final chapter. The development of partnership working requires a different set of skills. These include developing professional relationships with workers from a range of health and social welfare agencies. Mental health work is one of the key areas where such responses occur. Police officers feel that deinstitutionalisation was forcing them into the role of 'social workers' (Punch, 1979) or 'street corner psychiatrists' (Teplin, 1984).

There is a danger of assuming that these are new issues. There have always been overlaps between law enforcement and public health (Bartkowiak-Théron and Asquith, 2016). Lombroso's (2012) Social Darwinism is a medical model of criminality. The formation of the modern state has its roots in responses to plague and other public health concerns. The COVID-19 pandemic has emphasised again this link (De Waal, 2020). Police officers can have a key role to play in situations in which individuals are experiencing some sort of crisis related to mental health problems. The issue has risen up the policy agenda during the period of welfare retrenchment. Police involvement in mental health work has to be viewed as part of their role in wider community safety and the protection of vulnerable people.

Wolff (2005) argues that the police have always had what might be termed a 'quasi social work' role. This is vital work but mental health work does not fit easily with aspects of 'cop culture' that Reiner (1992b) identifies. For example, there is often not an immediate response in terms of action that can be taken. Policing is action and outcome orientated. There is not an immediate intervention that will resolve the underlying factors that create a mental health crisis. It is an area that creates challenges for police services (Carey, 2001; Lurigio and Watson, 2010). These challenges are both individual and organisational. Wood et al's (2011) review of trends in the UK, Canada and the US concluded that the same issues arise across the countries: a combination of reduced psychiatric provision and poorly funded community services has led to increased pressure on police officers who often receive little mental health training. Police officers, particularly in urban areas, deal with incidents that relate in some way or another to mental illness on an almost daily basis. Lord Adebowale (2013) carried out an inquiry into policing and mental health work in the Metropolitan Police Service. The inquiry was initially into the death of Sean Rigg in police custody in 2008. Rigg, who had a history of mental illness, died after being restrained by the police. They had been called by support staff at the accommodation where Rigg was living as he has been behaving erratically. Lord Adebowale broadened the scope of his inquiry because of the level of police work that was mental health related. He concluded that mental health is 'core police business'. This should be taken to mean that dealing with individuals experiencing mental distress is a key feature of the working week of most police officers. In 2015, when giving evidence to the Home Affairs Select Committee, Sir Peter Fahy, then Chief Constable of Greater Manchester, described mental health as the 'number one' issue for frontline officers.

The College of Policing

The College of Policing was established in 2012 as a professional body to lead and develop an evidence base. The Coalition government's austerity policies led to a reduction in police numbers. As police officer numbers were declining the demands on the police were increasing. This included mental health work (Caveney et al, 2020). The College produced an analysis of the demands that are placed on an average force for one day. This work shows the wide variety of demands that are placed on the police and the impact of mental health work. The analysis showed that recorded crime and incidents have been decreasing over the past decade. However, this is not true for all crimes. There has been an increase in cybercrime, including fraud. In this period, there was an increase in the number of reported rapes. The reporting of historical offences has been a factor here. The investigation of such offences demands more resources because of the need to analyse social media accounts and personal data.

Measuring demand in police mental health work

Attempts to identify and accurately measure mental health work in policing result in a focus on crisis situations or mental health emergencies. This focus obscures the reality that people with mental health problems, like all citizens, can potentially encounter the police in a wide range of circumstances. The focus on crisis intervention additionally obscures the fact that people with mental health problems are more likely to be victims of crime. It is important to emphasise that policing is a complex, dynamic and multifaceted task. The role clearly involves the immediate response to crime and the apprehension and the arrest of offenders. However, there are many other tasks or police responses that are not directly related to offending. Representations of policing in the media and popular culture focus more on dramatic car chases and high profile crime (Cummins et al, 2014). The advent of reality TV programmes such as *24 Hours in Police Custody* have seen these welfare aspects of policing being given greater coverage. Such programmes tend to follow a narrative that emphasises that police are increasingly and reluctantly drawn into supporting people in crisis because of failings in other areas.

Mental health work is one aspect of policing demand. To manage demand generally, the police have introduced the 101 phone line for incidents that do not require an emergency response. However, one of the problems here is that for individuals making the call the issue is often perceived as an emergency. Despite these attempts to control demand, and media reports of inappropriate calls and the highlighting of reduction in officer numbers, it remains difficult for police forces to control this aspect of their work. The College of Policing (2015) in its discussion of the broader pressures on police forces identified several key factors. In 2013/2014, there were 3.7 million crimes recorded by the police. This represented a 21 per cent fall since 2008/2009. As the College of Policing (2015) report points out, there was a 14 per cent fall in the number of police officers in the period 2010–2014 which saw the first wave of retrenchment under the coalition government's austerity policies. While crime was falling overall, there were rises in certain areas. For example, sexual offences rose by 20 per cent. Such offences are demanding to investigate. A number of these cases were historical, making the investigation more complex still. In all types of cases, the increased use of social media and CCTV mean that police officers are potentially dealing with more material that requires time-consuming examination.

One of the key themes in the discussion of the increased demands that the police face in this area is the impact of the cuts in other services. There are two elements to this.

There is a strong feeling among police officers that they are 'picking up the pieces' – this was the subtitle of a report by Her Majesty's Inspectorate of Constabulary and Fire and Rescue Services (HMICFRS) (2018) – for failing community mental health services. This can be seen in social media posts about whether it is appropriate or 'the police's job' to respond in certain situations – for example if a patient is missing from a mental health ward. The second element is the frustration that police officers feel in either delays or what are viewed as inadequate responses from mental health professionals. Mental health crises often build to a point where individuals, families and carers seek emergency support. The HMICFRS (2018) report notes that the peak period for mental health related calls to the police is Monday to Friday, 3pm–6pm. There are several possible explanations for this. The increase in calls in the late afternoon might be due to people with mental health problems experiencing disturbed sleep patterns, then waking later in the day and seeking help. The HMICFRS (2018) report also suggests that this increase indicates that as other agencies are finishing work or switching to limited out of hours office cover then the police are contacted. There is a further spike in demand between 5pm and 10pm on Saturdays and Sundays. These spikes seem to indicate that when gaps in community based mental health services are felt most keenly 999 calls will increase. *Picking up the pieces* suggests that 10 per cent of mental health related calls with concerns for the safety of an individual come from other mental health agencies.

Demand is not simply about the number of calls, though this is clearly important. Not all calls are as demanding and complex as others or require an immediate response. Lord Adebowale (2013) found that, in 2012, the Metropolitan Police Service (MPS) received 61,258 calls involving a mental health issue of some sort. This is an average of over 160 a day. In the same period, it took about 40,000 calls that related to robberies and nearly 15,000 calls that related to sexual offences. A significant number of these calls took place outside of office hours, so at night or at the weekend, when it is even more difficult to access support for people in crisis. As already noted, people with mental health issues are witnesses, victims of crime or suspects as well as coming into contact with the police in crisis. A survey of MPS officers indicated 'daily or regular' encounters with victims (39 per cent), witnesses (23 per cent) and suspects (48 per cent) with mental health conditions, and 67 per cent encountered unusual behaviour, attributed to drugs and/or alcohol. In addition, the HMICFRS (2018) report highlights that the response to mental health related incidents differ from other areas of policing. The average response time was slower but such incidents then were likely to require more resources than other areas. More officers are likely to be involved. The police often need to liaise with mental health and triage services.

It has been difficult for police forces to obtain an accurate picture of the demands that mental health related incidents generate. There is no statutory requirement for forces to provide data on mental health incidents apart from section 136 MHA detentions. The collection of data on the use of section 136 MHA was, until recent improvements, very patchy (Cummins and Edmondson, 2016). The same can be said for data concerning PACE police interviews of adults that take place with an AA present.

Models of policing

The increasing concerns about the police role in mental health work has resulted in the development of new models of police response. These models have been developed as a result of national and local circumstances – often in response to a critical incident or the death of a person with mental health problems following police contact. Lamb et al (2002) identify three possible models of police response to people in mental health. Mental health crisis is not used in any clinical sense here. The models are:

- specialist trained officers;
- joint police and mental health teams; and
- phone triage or a system that allows officers to access relevant health information and records.

Specialist police officers

The Crisis Intervention Team (CIT) based in Memphis (Compton et al, 2008) was established in 1988 following an incident when the Memphis Police shot dead a man who was suffering from a psychotic illness. CIT officers deal with mental health emergencies but also act in a consultancy role to fellow officers. To become a CIT officer, personnel have to undergo intensive mental health awareness work as well as training in de-escalation techniques. The key factors in the success of the CIT model are the increased police confidence in dealing with these situations and the 'no refusal policy' that is established with the local mental health units (Watson et al, 2008).

Joint police and mental health teams

There are a several approaches to the provision of a joint police and mental health professional response. The most well-established of these models are to be found in the US and Canada. An example of a joint approach is Car 87 in Vancouver. The Car 87 project is jointly funded between the police and local mental health services. In addition to a joint response it also provides a mental health phone triage service.

Triage

Triage is a well-established concept within general nursing and medicine. In this process, an early assessment allows for individuals at accident and emergency to be treated speedily in the most appropriate setting. This process also allows for the more efficient allocation of medical resources. Mental health triage has come to be used as a short-hand for a number of models of joint services with mental health staff and policing. These systems share the same aims as triage in that they combine some element of assessment with a recognition that individuals need to access the most appropriate services in a timely fashion. In addition, these models of service provision seek to improve officers' confidence in decision making in the context of mental health.

In England and Wales, the Cleveland Street Triage team was established in 2012. This is also a joint health and police funded project that ensures that mental health nurses are available to carry out assessments when police are called to an incident. Studies of phone triage systems, such as Sands et al (2013), have concentrated on the effective management of mental health crises within psychiatric services. These studies highlight the advantages of such approaches both in terms of clinical outcomes but also the more effective use of resources. Policing requires officers to exercise a considerable amount of discretion and individual judgement. This is true in all areas of policing but seems particularly relevant in the area of mental health. Variables that influence decision making are the nature of the incident, the available resources and the training and experience of the officers involved. It can be argued that triage systems may increase the range of resources available to the police (and others) and are a means of confirming and developing individual skills and confidence in this field.

The narrative framing of police mental health work

Frederick et al's study (2018) is based on a scoping review of 92 articles published between 2000 and 2017 that examined issues related to mental health and policing. The authors note that there has been an expansion of the research in this field. Alongside this increased research interest, there has been an expansion in the variety of terminology and frames used in debates. Despite this broadening interest, the impact of deinstitutionalisation remains the dominant frame for the discussion of these issues. The policy of deinstitutionalisation began over 50 years ago – this is not to say that its impact should not be considered. Frederick et al (2018) argue that the dominant narrative of deinstitutionalisation obscures the impact of more recent social and welfare policies (Cummins, 2018b). The dominant deinstitutionalisation framing narrative also has the effect of constructing this issue in terms of the difficulties it raises for the police. This means that the impact of police involvement on service users has been marginalised. There has been comparatively little research on the experiences of mental health services users when they have contact with the police. Riley et al's (2011) study of service-users' experience of being detained under section 136 of the MHA, while demonstrating that officers responded in a compassionate way to those in distress, showed that overall, this was perceived as a custodial rather than a therapeutic intervention. Foley and Cummins' (2018) analysis of the reporting of sexual assaults and violence on mental health inpatient units highlighted the additional barriers that victims faced in bringing forward allegations. Service-users felt that allegations would be dismissed because of their mental state or even seen as a symptom of illness.

The dominance of the deinstitutionalisation narrative also seems to imply that the solution to these issues is to return to the previous system. The asylums of the mid-20th century will not return. This is due to a combination of factors including fiscal concerns and the recognition of the abuses of institutionalised psychiatry. The police have always had some role in the responses to people experiencing a mental health crisis. It is, to my mind at least, difficult if not impossible to manage a system where this would not be the case.

The role of the police in mental health work has become the focus of increased debate. Concerns focus on the increase demands on the police and whether officers have the skills to respond appropriately to people in crisis. These concerns developed initially due to the impact of deinstitutionalisation. These have been heightened in England and Wales by the impact of austerity. The number of police officers has fallen while the demands have increased. Within the organisational culture of policing, there is the potential for mental health work to be seen as 'not proper policing'. The image of policing in the media and popular culture is very much dominated by responses to serious and violent crime. This brings with it a sort of glamour somewhat at odds with the day to day reality of policing (Cummins et al, 2014). There is a danger that mental health work will be seen as having a lower status and organisational priority.

Responding to a mental health emergency or other situations involving a vulnerable adult requires a different set of skills. However, there are core skills that police officers use – critical thinking, communication skills, information gathering, negotiation and decision making. These are complex issues which are not easily resolved. This is a source of particular frustration for officers, who are often outcome-focused (Reiner, 1992b). The most complex mental health related work is not going to be 'solved' by police intervention. Such an intervention will deal, however imperfectly, with an immediate crisis. Long-standing complex issues require long-term solutions.

Conclusion

Bittner (1967, 1970) notes that policing is a complex task that requires the exercise of considerable discretion and individual judgement. It is much more than the detection of crime and apprehending offenders. This research supports the argument that a significant proportion of police work is not directed towards crime. Bittner (1974) described a police officer as 'Florence Nightingale in pursuit of Willie Sutton' – Sutton was a famous bank robber. In the management of public order, arrest and custody should be viewed as being at one end of a continuum. In Teplin's (1984) seminal study of policing and mental illness, she used the term 'mercy booking' to describe the situation where the police arrest an individual because they felt that this would ensure that a vulnerable person was given food and shelter – even if it was in custody.

Morabito (2007) argues that police decision making is more complex than is allowed for in these situations. She argues that police decision making is shaped by a number of variables. These are termed 'horizons of context'. This model provides a tool for the analysis of the decisions that officers make. In Morabito's model, there are three variable contexts. The scenic context refers to the range of the community resources that are available, including the range of voluntary and statutory mental health services, access to training for officers and the working relationships between agencies. The discretion that officers can exercise is clearly limited by the range of services available. If community services are limited, then custody becomes regrettably a more likely outcome.

Morabito (2007) outlines two other 'horizons of context', which she terms *temporal* and *manipulative*. In this model, temporal refers to the individual and manipulative to the actual incident. There will be some incidents – for example in the rare cases when a violent crime has been committed – where the police for evidential and public protection reasons will have little alternative but to take the person into custody. At the other end of the scale, a very experienced officer dealing with a minor incident involving an individual they know well, will have much greater scope to exercise discretion. The scope will increase in areas where there are greater community mental health resources. As Morabito concludes, there is a tendency to oversimplify the decision making processes that police officers use in these complex and demanding situations. The local service, social and environmental contexts are thus vitally important.

In February 2014, the Crisis Care Concordat was signed by more than 20 national organisations in England in a bid to drive up standards of care for people in mental health crisis. The Concordat sought to build on other announcements on mental health care. These have included liaison and diversion schemes, for example placing mental health professionals in police custody and court settings to help identify mental health problems in offenders as early as possible. In addition, a number of areas have developed versions of street triage schemes where mental health clinicians – typically trained nurses – accompany police officers when making emergency responses to people suffering from a mental health crisis. The nurses may also advise and support officers by telephone. As College of Policing Chief Executive Chief Constable Alex Marshall stated: 'The Concordat is a strong statement of intent of how the police, mental health services, social work services and ambulance professionals will work together to make sure that people who need immediate mental health support at a time of crisis get the right services when they need them' (College of Policing, 2015).

Wood et al's (2011) review of trends in the UK, Canada and the US concludes that the same issues arise across the countries: a combination of reduced psychiatric provision and poorly funded community services has led to increased pressure on police officers who often receive little or no specific mental health training. Police officers, particularly in urban areas, deal with incidents that relate in some way or another to mental illness on an almost daily basis. It is likely that the police will always be 'first responders' to many incidents. The key, then, is how the police are supported by wider community mental health agencies to ensure the response is appropriate. This is to ensure that individuals are safe but also to support police officers to make informed, professional and defensible decisions. There will always be cases where an individual who is mentally ill will be taken into police custody because they have committed or are suspected of a violent crime. These are the minority. Police officers need training in mental health awareness to increase their confidence in decision making. In addition, there needs to be more effective liaison and joint working between mental health services and the police to ensure that individuals receive support from the most appropriate services in a timely fashion. Lord Adebowale (2013) concluded that mental health is core police business. There are a number of models of triage that have been have developed in response to local organisational, demographic and other factors – for example as a response to a tragic incident or the commitment of individuals. It would be foolish to try to be very prescriptive in developing models of triage. However, all these schemes have two key features – the improved training for officers and improved liaison with mental health services. These elements are vital whatever the nature of the mental health crisis or incident that is being addressed. There are clear challenges for police officers in mental health work. It is important to recognise that officers respond to these complex and demanding situations – often with little specialist support – to ensure the safety and welfare of vulnerable citizens.

Further reading

College of Policing (2015) Mental vulnerability and illness. Available at: https://www.app.college.police.uk/app-content/mental-health/mental-vulnerability-and-illness/

Cummins, I. (2020a) Policing, vulnerability and mental health. In J.L.M. McDaniel, K. Moss and K.G. Pease (eds) *Policing and mental health: theory, policy and practice*. Abingdon: Routledge, pp 182–200.

Her Majesty's Inspectorate of Constabulary and Fire and Rescue Services (2018) Policing and mental health: picking up the pieces. Available at: www.justiceinspectorates.gov.uk/hmicfrs/wp-content/uploads/policing-and-mental-health-picking-up-the-pieces.pdf

Lane, R. (2019) 'I'm a police officer not a social worker or mental health nurse': online discourses of exclusion and resistance regarding mental health-related police work. *Journal of Community & Applied Social Psychology*, 29(5), 429–442.

McDaniel, J.L. (2019) Reconciling mental health, public policing and police accountability. *The Police Journal*, 92(1), 72–94.

National Police Chiefs Council (2020) National strategy on policing and mental health. National Police Chiefs Council. Available at: www.npcc.police.uk/Mental%20Health/Nat%20Strat%20Final%20v2%2026%20Feb%202020.pdf

Thomas, S. (2020) Critical essay: fatal encounters involving people experiencing mental illness. *Salus Journal*, 8(2), 100–116.

5

Policing and stress

Introduction

This chapter will examine the causes of and response to occupational stress that is inherent within modern policing. It identifies the potential causes of stress that are embedded in the policing role. Some of these relate to the nature of the work. For example, it is clear that responding to traumatised people who have been victims of violence or investigating sexual offences will inevitably impact on professionals carrying out this work. Alongside this, in common with other public sector professionals, police officers feel overwhelmed by the bureaucratic demands that come with the role. Having outlined the potential causes of stress, the chapter examines how these issues have been and are represented in modern drama. These representations reflect changing attitudes to stress. Policing is inherently stressful. There seems to be little that can be done to tackle some of the inherent causes of that stress or limit exposure to traumatic events (Gershon et al, 2009). The result is that stress can come to be regarded as an occupational hazard, something that all officers are likely to experience. There is a danger that such an approach fails to recognise the cumulative impact of working as a police officer (Tuckey and Scott, 2013). There is a growing literature that challenges these engrained notions and seeks to develop services to respond to them. Police forces recognise that the welfare and wellbeing of staff is a major issue that requires an organisational response. It is important to recognise that there have been significant policy developments in this area.

Policing and stress

Considerations of stress and policing have to be placed in the wider context of developments in the public services. Unusually for a Conservative led government, the coalition government did not exempt the police from the broader cuts that austerity introduced (Cummins, 2018a). For example, in the period 2010–2015, the budget of Greater Manchester Police (GMP) was reduced by around £130 million. The number of police officers halved. At the 2020 General Election, the Conservative Manifesto included a commitment to the recruitment of 20,000 new police officers. As many commentators noted, this would bring police numbers back to roughly the level before austerity. One overlooked factor here is the impact on organisations of the loss of experienced staff. Experienced staff play a key role in the mentoring and development of new recruits. The loss of experienced staff also means that the organisational memory is compromised or lost alongside the informal working relationships and links that staff develop with colleagues from social services, health and other welfare organisations. These changes mean that the police service has faced a period of significant change. Alongside the reduction in police budgets (Sigurdsson and Dhani, 2010), there have been changes to the employment terms and conditions for officers and staff (Winsor, 2012). These changes have taken place in and contributed to a very different policing environment. Reduced police numbers are responding to a range of new demands in a radically different working environment (Finnegan, 2015; Weinfass, 2015). Change on such scale is bound to generate organisational and individual stress. Individuals perform best in an environment where there is security – in terms of their employment but also in their role and position within the organisation.

Policing has undergone significant organisational change. Alongside this, police forces have come under attack from traditional supporters in the right-wing media, which views the police as abandoning its traditional approach to embrace the wider diversity agenda. Critics see this as coming at the expense of the proper police role of protecting the public. At the same time as these developments, there has been an increased focus on the psychological wellbeing of officers. This is seen as further evidence that the traditional police role has been corrupted. From this increasingly marginalised perspective, the recognition of response to stress is a modern affectation.

There has been an increasing focus on the psychological impact on officers of facing the difficult situations that are a daily part of policing. Police officers face extreme situations such as the aftermath of serious road traffic accidents or murder and death (Henry, 2004). One element here is that the police have no control over these events. An officer at the start of the working day has no real idea what they might encounter. This is part of the attraction of the role – alongside serving the community and the excitement that some police work entails. However, it is important to recognise that these elements can also act as stressors. The potential negative impacts can be psychological and physical or both. They include stress, anxiety and in extreme cases suicide (Costa et al, 2019). In addition, research indicates that the stress of the police role can lead to psychical exhaustion, compassion fatigue and even moral suffering (Papazoglou et al, 2017, 2020; Violanti et al, 2019). The police work in an environment which requires officer to be hypervigilant. There are long periods of mundane work while on duty. One of the largest complaints from police officers is the sheer volume of paperwork and bureaucracy (Violanti, 1996). This complaint is common across public service settings such as health and social care. The dominant media image of the police officer is the assertive, dynamic thief-taker battling internal bureaucracy as well as criminal elements to keep society safe.

Police officers face high, even extremes, levels of workplace stress. Some of the causes of this are deeply rooted within police work. Attitudes to mental health are changing but historically, the macho culture of policing has meant that these issues have not been openly discussed or acknowledged. A working or organisational culture where emotional reactions to difficult situations are seen as signs of 'weakness' make it difficult, if not impossible, for officers to raise these issues. Policing culture on patrol can be very similar to that outlined in the classic ethnographic studies of the 1970s (Reiner, 1992b, 2010). Attitudes to workplace stress are part of this phenomenon. Acknowledging any personal problem is still seen as a sign of weakness – it is part of the job so you have to get used to it. This is not to deny that there have been significant changes. It simply recognises that there are still steps that need to be taken. It is also important to acknowledge that policing is not alone in needing to shift organisational and personal attitudes in this field. The same applies to other emergency services, the military and social work. What these professions have in common is that staff deal with the extremes of human experience.

Policing has become a more complex and demanding job. This has led to officers experiencing increased levels of work related stress (Queiros et al, 2020). Job stress leads to individual distress and poor performance (Baldwin et al, 2019). Individual stress has an impact on personal relationships and family life (Griffin and Sun, 2018). As in other areas, individuals develop their own 'coping strategies'. These are patterns of behaviour that can be identified in other professional settings. These can include alcohol and substance misuse and the avoidance of tasks (Kamarudin et al, 2018). Working excessive hours may be seen as inevitable in emergency situations but being a 'workalcoholic' is actually a response to stress. It also inevitably impacts on performance. Long-term experience of stress can lead to burnout (Rosa et al, 2015). One of the strengths of the police is the commit to the 'police family'. However, stress and other factors can contribute to lead to unacceptable attitudes and conduct such as the use of excessive force (Neely and Cleveland, 2011).

To the outside observer, the most stressful elements of the police officer's role would appear to be the threat of having to deal with physical violence or responding to people experiencing extreme trauma. However, police officers identified the major causes of stress as the bureaucratic side of the job (Violanti, 2010). In this study, officers downplayed aspects of the job which outsiders might view as the most stressful. It is possible that this is further evidence of a 'stress denying' organisational culture. Stress has long-term physical and emotional impacts. The police recruit fit and healthy individuals but they have higher rates of early retirement and a lower life expectancy than the wider population (Violanti et al, 1998).

One aspect of the increased interest in the problems of workplace stress in the past two decades has been the concepts of 'vicarious trauma' and 'burnout'. Symptoms of workplace stress can include: depression, anxiety, poor sleep, headaches, decrease in sexual interest, withdrawal, irritability, poor communication, drug and alcohol abuse, low self-esteem and difficulty in decision making. Vicarious trauma is a way of exploring the impact of working with traumatised individuals. Initial work (McCann and Pearlmann, 1990) was carried out with counsellors who were supporting the victims of sexual violence. Vicarious trauma is seen as a cumulative process where the worker, though not subject to the same traumatic events, begins to exhibit symptoms that are similar to post-traumatic stress disorder (PTSD). Adams and Riggs (2008) outline several possible symptoms including anxiety/depression, somatic symptoms, emotional numbing and the blurring of personal and professional boundaries. The idea of vicarious trauma was subsequently applied to other professions. The concept has also been used to explore the long-term effects of police work. The idea of vicarious trauma explicitly acknowledges that there is a possible emotional and psychological cost to supporting those who have undergone extreme sexual and physical trauma. The original study of vicarious trauma took place in an environment where one would assume that staff were much more aware of emotional issues. Even in this environment, it was difficult to support staff, and as previously stated, occupational culture in the police force often mitigates against an open acknowledgement of these stresses (Sackmann, 1991).

MIND (2015) carried out a survey of police officers, fire brigade, ambulance and search and rescue staff. Over a thousand police officers took part in the survey. Of the police respondents, 91 per cent experienced symptoms of stress including low mood and poor mental health. The police were the group in the survey with the highest levels of poor mental health. In this study, bureaucratic issues such as workload, organisational and policy changes, as well as management initiatives, were seen as greater stress factors than responding to traumatic incidents. This emphasises that the organisational context can have a huge influence – often greater than the nature of the day-to-day work.

The Police Federation of England and Wales surveyed all officers in England and Wales (Houdmont and Elliott-Davies, 2016). The importance of the issue was reflected in the fact that there were over 16,000 responses. Of these, 80 per cent of officers indicated that they experienced feelings of stress such as low mood or anxiety. The survey was repeated in 2018 and more than 18,000 officers responded. The results were remarkably similar: 79.3 per cent of officers indicated that they had experience feelings of stress and poor mental health at some point in the previous year, and 94.2 per cent of officers indicated that stress had been caused or exacerbated by work. The demands of work and the inability to maintain a sense of work/life balance were key factors (Elliott-Davies, 2019).

All roles in policing have the potential to be stressful – the organisational factors apply whether an officer is a road traffic officer or investigating homicide. Having acknowledged this, there are clearly areas of police work that are more demanding. These include areas such as domestic violence and abuse, child sexual abuse, child pornography and homicide (Roach et al, 2017, 2018). As one might imagine, cases involving children and the feelings that these generate can have a particularly profound impact (Roach et al, 2017, 2018). The impact of responding to traumatised victims or parents and relatives in cases of child abduction or murder can lead to symptoms of PTSD such as flashbacks or fatigue. These can continue even when officers have retired from the police service (Violanti, 1996). It is not unusual for an experienced or retired homicide detective to focus on one case from their experience (Roach et al, 2018). The impact of psychological distress can manifest itself in forms of disengagement and the development of deeply cynical and pessimistic views of policing and an individual's role in it. In the US, suicide among police has become a serious problem with officers often using their own service handgun to end their lives (Costa et al, 2019). One of the major criticisms of the representation of policing in drama is that it rarely engages in a sensitive way with the personal impact of these sorts of investigations (Cummins et al, 2014).

Burnout

Terms such as burnout, vicarious trauma, PTSD and compassion fatigue have entered the popular lexicon. It is a positive that these areas are more openly discussed. However, it is important to recognise that such terms have a technical usage that is not always the same as when the term is used in popular discourse. Freudenberger (1974) first used the term 'staff burnout' to describe the negative impact that he and his colleagues felt working with problem drug users in New York. The term captures both the physical and emotional impact that such work can have. Maslach (1976, 1982) developed the term 'burnout' as a way of explaining the way that stress can drain an individual of motivation. Maslach (1976, 1982) highlighted the way that staff in caring professions, who were working in emotionally demanding situations or with traumatised individuals, were placed under psychological pressure. This then impacted on the staff but also the way they carried out the role. The key symptom of burnout is a form of emotional exhaustion – though physical exhaustion also occurs. Other symptoms or indicators include irritability and low morale. Burnout can also lead to poor work performance or the avoidance of challenging situations. The emotional impact of burnout leads to a loss of self-esteem and the development of pessimistic and cynical attitudes to the role that the professional is undertaking. Burnout is usually thought of as cumulative experience, the result of a dealing with a series of traumatic experiences (Kohan and Mazmanian, 2003). There is a danger that this build up is missed. Signs of burnout might also be seen as 'natural' or inevitable given the role. For example, Perez et al (2010), in a small study of officers involved in the investigation of child pornography cases, found over 50 per cent showed signs of emotional exhaustion. The finding in itself might not be too surprising given the nature of the work. However, this should not obscure the potential impact on an individual officer's mental health and the ripple effects this can have on his/her family.

Research into the experience of burnout among police officers has sought to examine the impact of individual characteristics of officers and job conditions. It is important to emphasise that if one focuses on individuals there is the danger that organisational factors are marginalised. It is a short step from this to blaming individuals or seeing burnout as the result of individual failings. The research findings are inconsistent. McCarty et al (2007) found little difference in burnout between males and females. However, other research has suggested that female officers experienced higher levels of stress than their male colleagues (McCarty and Skogan, 2012). In the study, McCarty and Skogan (2012) found that Black female officers experienced higher rates of burnout than their White female colleagues (McCarty and Skogan, 2012). This was linked to their doubly marginalised status within policing as Black women. Another theme in research has been the attempts to identify those factors that contribute to individuals being 'resilient'. Again, there is a need for caution here to avoid slipping into victim blaming. Just as organisations can be resilient, they can also be dysfunctional. However resilient an individual might be they cannot necessarily overcome the problems that such organisational factors create. This can be viewed as a way of understanding those factors that mean that some individuals are able to carry on and not experience burnout. Resiliency can be seen as the way that individuals and agencies are able to draw upon a range of individual and organisational resources to meet the challenges of a critical incident or the ongoing demands of the role (Paton et al, 2013). Burnout is the result of exceptional and chronic job stress (Schaufeli, 2017). It is often viewed as a response to the cumulative impact of ongoing stressful factors. Burnout has become endemic in the modern workplace.

Vicarious trauma

Vicarious trauma impacts on those who are working with traumatised victims. For example, workers and counsellors in rape crisis centres will be working with individuals who have been subjected to the sexual violence. The victims' accounts are frequently dismissed. Vicarious trauma is the effect of hearing such accounts – a worker becomes traumatised even though they have not experienced the event themselves (McCann and Pearlman, 1990). It is important to emphasise that this vicarious trauma does not describe the normal response or feelings of empathy that one might have when working with a traumatised victim. It is the cumulative impact on the individual worker of being exposed to these accounts of trauma or witnessing the impact on victims. Vicarious trauma results in significant changes – these can include emotional exhaustion, irritability, vulnerability and cynicism. McCann and Pearlman (1990) highlighted that vicarious trauma led to workers changing their view of the world. It also had a corrosive impact on work/life balance and personal relationships. Vicarious trauma can lead to flashbacks and other intrusive thoughts (McCann and Pearlman, 1990). Vicarious trauma can lead to workers losing the positive motivation that drove them to take up the role in the first place. For example, workers may lose sight of the individual and their traumatic experiences or feel that no interventions can be successful. Vicarious trauma like other stress related conditions is an inherent risk in policing – there may be roles where officers are at greater risk than others. There are issues of professional responsibility here – all professionals have a duty to recognise any factors that might have an impact on their ability to carry out their role. However, there is a danger that this becomes a way to blame individuals rather than examining the structural issues that contribute. In policing and other professions, there are deeply entrenched cultural and organisational issues that act as barriers to individuals seeking help (Jetelina et al, 2020).

Post-traumatic stress disorder

PTSD is a term that has come into common usage over the past 50 years. It has become a common theme in film and drama but is also used in popular discourse. These usages can conflate PTSD with other forms of mental distress but also, unintentionally, minimise the nature and potential impact of the disorder. The diagnosis of PTSD has its roots in the experiences of GIs in the Vietnam War. War and its impact have played an influential role in the wider development of psychiatry. For example, the identification of 'shell-shock' among officers in the First World War led to a change in attitudes and a wider recognition that mental illness was experienced across all social classes (Cummins, 2020d). Symptoms such as flashbacks, upsetting memories and anxiety following a traumatic event are recognised features of PTSD. Soldiers and civilians in conflicts had experienced these symptoms in many forms before PTSD was formally recognised as a mental health condition in 1980, only five years after the end of the Vietnam War. The initial focus of PTSD was on the experiences of soldiers – Vietnam veterans campaigned for it to be recognised as a mental health condition. Since that period, there has been a recognition that the initial trauma covers a wider range of experiences including being the victim of sexual assault and violent crime. The key phrase in terms of the definition of trauma is an event that is outside the range of usual human experience and that would be markedly distressing. Thus trauma begins in the experience of war but then moves to a much broader recognition. Not all those are who exposed to these traumatic events go on to experience the symptoms of PTSD.

One of the fundamental elements in a diagnosis of PTSD is that the person has experienced a trauma. Trauma really refers to an event that is outside the normal range of human experience. If an individual develops PTSD, the traumatic event is re-experienced or revisited. This might be triggered by a range of stimuli – sights, sounds, smells or revisiting a place where trauma occurred or having a similar experience. The experience of PTSD includes recurrent and intrusive thoughts or nightmares. Flashbacks or dissociative episodes are not uncommon. Those who experience PTSD often have difficulty sleeping alongside a range of other symptoms such as poor concentration or hypervigilance. Hypervigilance is a state of increased alertness. It can lead to individuals constantly looking for potential threats or dangers or restricting the daily lives in some way to minimise perceived dangers. A person needs to experience symptoms of PTSD for more than a month and for these symptoms to cause significant distress or impact on an individual's normal ability to function for a diagnosis to be made.[1]

The impact of stress and organisational responses

This section will discuss recent research about the impact of stress, including a consideration of its economic cost. It will then go on to examine recent developments that show that policing, alongside other Blue Light organisations, is taking work-related stress much more seriously.

As already noted, one of the possible signs of stress is actually working excessive hours or not taking sick leave. MIND (2020) found that emergency workers were more likely to experience mental health problems than the general workforce. However these workers were less likely to report them and take time off (MIND, 2020). This may be partly explained by an organisational or working culture that does not recognise work-related stress as legitimate. The Blue Light programme was established to tackle this stigma around mental health in emergency services. It offers support and interventions to improve mental health and wellbeing. In 2019, the College of Policing launched the National Police Wellbeing Service. This development was financed by £7.5 million funding from the Home Office. Oscar Kilo is a joint College of Policing and Public

Health England initiative. Oscar Kilo produces online resources to support mental health and wellbeing. Even five years ago, it would have been hard to imagine that there would be this level of organisational and senior management commitment to tackling poor mental health and wellbeing across the workforce.

These developments are responses to a series of surveys and research that painted a picture of police officers struggling to maintain good mental health and wellbeing in the context of increasing demand and public service retrenchment. In MIND's 2015 study, 91 per cent of respondents had experienced symptoms such as stress or low mood, or poor sleep and appetite (MIND, 2015). The police service respondents reported the highest levels of personal mental health distress in a survey of emergency workers (MIND, 2015). In a survey of English and Welsh officers, 39 per cent reported high work-related stress levels (Houdmont and Elliott-Davies, 2016). These findings underline the stress-inducing nature of the 'first responder role'. There are two widely identified sources of stress – operational and organisational. In the organisational factors, the role and conduct of line managers has been identified as a key potential trigger of work-related stress.

The National Police Wellbeing Service (NPWS) has developed support and guidance for policing. It is recognised that to tackle work-related stress effectively, there needs to be a shift in organisational and cultural attitudes. In society generally, there is a much wider recognition of the potential impact of mental health problems including workplace stress and related issues. Senior managers and leaders need to set an example in this area alongside the establishment of robust policies and support systems for individual officers. The NPWS is available to all police forces in England and Wales. The following services are available:

- *Leadership for wellbeing*: the focus is on developing Executive Leaders and Line Managers to lead and manage organisations in ways that focus on wellbeing, and improve performance.
- *Individual resilience*: building individual resilience of officers and staff by developing their understanding of the causes of workplace stress and appropriate strategies and techniques to enhance personal wellbeing and improve their ability to support others.
- *Peer support for wellbeing*: delivering a national peer support model and network in order to provide the best care and support.
- *Psychological risk management*: high risk roles are screened for potential psychological trauma and wellbeing screening is available for all.
- *Trauma management*: providing a police-specific post-incident support and disaster management model of care for officers and staff.
- *Wellbeing at work*: occupational Health support, advice and liaison.

- *Mobile wellbeing outreach service*: providing access to wellbeing services at the place of work, in order to increase the opportunity to access wellbeing services.
- *Physical wellbeing*: including fitness mentoring and initiatives with police charities and collaborations with several UK universities.

Media representations of policing and stress

This section provides a brief introduction into media representations of policing. One of the most significant changes that has taken place is the foregrounding of issues such as police corruption but also the personal impact of policing on individuals. These trends have increased with the emergence of Nordic noir – detective fiction from writers such as Henning Mankell and his creation Wallander. In this genre, a recurrent theme is the 'broken by the job' police officer. Wallander is a prime example of this, an officer who has become world-weary and cynical, whose commitment to the job alienated him from his friends and family.

Police dramas have been a staple of film and TV schedules almost since the medium appeared. This popularity raises questions such as the potential influence on the public's view of policing, police officers and wider penal policy. Dyer (2002) sees entertainment as a form of escapism, as it offers the viewer a glimpse of a world outside of the everyday. The implication being that it will be more glamorous and exciting than the viewers' lives. The changes in the representation of policing can be used to track wider societal and cultural attitudes. The postwar consensus model of policing was captured by the long-running TV series *Dixon of Dock Green* (Allen et al, 1997; Dyer, 2005). Dixon came to represent an idealised, even for the 1950s, view of the police officer as the epitome of community values. Clarke (2005: 44) describes Dixon as a 'straight-backed, straight-laced, straight-thinking man with all the values of a boy scout'. The community-based setting, holistic nature of the work, caring approach and its early evening scheduling made it family viewing (Leishman and Mason, 2003). The viewers saw very little of Dixon's life outside of his work. There was no suggestion that he might be exposed to any form of psychological risk. Commentators, when holding their hands up in horror at the state of modern policing, often call for a return to the Dixon of Dock Green approach. In its values and storylines Dixon of Dock Green could hardly provide a sharper contrast to modern, particularly US-produced, police procedural dramas (Leishman and Mason, 2003).

The tensions between personal and professional ethics result in the emergence of the 'broken by the job' theme (Leishman and Mason, 2003). US programmes such as *NYPD Blue* (Bocho and Milch, 1993–2005) and *The Wire* (Simon, 2002–2008) seek to examine the role of the police in the postindustrial US city. Organisational and individual themes mesh. Office and institutional politics and bureaucracy are foregrounded. They are a source of major frustrations for officers.

Nordic noir (King and Cummins, 2014) has played a key role in the emergency of modern portrayals of policing. Robert Murphy's documentary, *Nordic noir: the story of Scandinavian crime fiction* (2010), argues that there are a number of factors which made the Nordic countries a suitable setting. The first is the physical surroundings and the weather, which create an atmosphere of darkness and foreboding. In addition, there is the conflict between the settings – countries which, from the outside, seem to have relatively low crime rates – and the brutal crimes being investigated.

Dark secrets are hidden within the apparent liberal Nordic model of politics. Alongside this, 'new' social issues such as immigration, asylum and an economic crisis create a challenge to the social democratic consensus. The result is a genre where the central characters, who are, typically, detectives, are worn down by the cares and stresses of the job and face a form of professional and existential crisis. Mankell's *Wallander* (Mankell, 2005–2013), perhaps the most popular Nordic detective in the UK, is the ultimate stressed-out, broken-by-the-job middle-aged detective. This is particularly the case in the Swedish TV series version. Wallander is a heavy drinker verging on alcoholism. He is divorced – police officers with long and happy marriages are a rarity in modern TV dramas. Wallander has a difficult relationship with his daughter, Linda, who is also a police officer. He is world-weary, absorbed by the job and clashing with bureaucratic pen-pushers but haunted by the horrors that he has witnessed.

Conclusion

It is clear that policing presents a unique set of challenges and circumstances that contribute to the increased risk of work-related stress. There has been a significant recent shift in social, cultural and organisational attitudes in this area. The impact of stress can lead to burnout. Burnout results in exhaustion and with it a reduced commitment or motivation to carry out the role. Other police officers suffering from work-related stress may have feelings of being overwhelmed by the role and the demands of the job. This can lead to conflict with families and loved ones. The wider impact of workplace stress can result in officers experiencing depression, anxiety and poor psychical health. In extreme cases, police officers may reach a point where they end their own life. The promotion of good mental health is an organisational priority but should also be seen as a wider commitment to individual staff. There is a great deal of positive work going on in this area. It could be argued that policing is ahead of other professions that face similar challenges. The nature of police work is not going to change significantly in that it will always involve the response to traumatic events of one form or another. Organisational culture can and is changing.

Further reading

Freudenberger, H.J. (1974) Staff burn-out. *Journal of Social Issues*, 30(1), 159–165.

Henry, V.E. (2004) *Death work: police, trauma, and the psychology of survival.* Oxford: Oxford University Press.

Houdmont, J. and Elliott-Davies, M. (2016) *Police Federation of England and Wales 2016 officer demand, capacity, and welfare survey.* Initial report, descriptive results.

Houdmont, J., Elliott-Davies, M. and Donnelly, J. (2018) Leaveism in English and Welsh police forces: baseline reference values. *Occupational Medicine*, 68(9), 593–599.

Kohan, A. and Mazmanian, D. (2003) Police work, burnout, and pro-organizational behavior: a consideration of daily work experiences. *Criminal Justice and Behavior*, 30(5), 559–583.

McCarty, W.P. and Skogan, W.G. (2012) Job-related burnout among civilian and sworn police personnel. *Police Quarterly*, 16(1), 66–84.

Roach, J., Sharratt, K., Cartwright, A. and Skou Roer, T. (2018) Cognitive and emotional stressors of child homicide investigations on UK and Danish police investigators. *Homicide Studies*, 22(3), 296–320.

6

A comparative research study of mental health triage

Alice Park

Introduction

This chapter will contextualise the role of the police where they encounter those experiencing mental distress by drawing on qualitative interview and observational data from a study which explored mental health triage. Mental health triage is an intervention implemented across England and Wales that pairs mental health professionals with police staff. Drawing on the perspectives of frontline police staff, and mental health professionals who work closely with them as part of the intervention, this chapter will give an overview of the mental health related work police staff can encounter on the frontline, and the dilemmas they face in their everyday work.

This chapter will first explore the policy context of mental health, policing and mental health triage, highlighting issues around mental health demand, multiagency collaboration, training for the police, decision making and what research has been conducted so far. This will be followed by an outline of the study including detail about the setting, recruitment and data analysis. The findings from this study will then outline the perceived demand placed on the police in relation to mental health work and what participants described as the role of the police here. The specific challenges around interagency working, the types of work the police do, as well as perceptions around training, knowledge and decision making will also be highlighted. Finally the discussion will consider wider questions around responsibility and the police role in mental health provision in the UK going forward.

Background

As has been discussed throughout the chapters in this book, the role of the police in mental health work is well recognised. The main concerns centre around issues of mental health related demand, multiagency collaboration and police knowledge, which can also be seen as the drivers for the inception of mental health triage. Mental health triage involves trained mental health professionals supporting the police where they encounter mental health related incidents, here advice may be given over the phone, or police may be supported in person. There are numerous approaches to mental health triage across Organisation for Economic Co-operation and Development countries, including differences in the personnel of the teams, their training, as well as activity during and after the triage encounter (see Puntis et al, 2018; Park et al, 2019 for an overview).

Demand

Discussions relating to the demand placed on the police force by those experiencing mental health issues often centre on the concern that it is ever increasing and is an inappropriate use of police time and resources (House of Commons Home Affairs Committee, 2015). Past estimates of the demand placed on the police by those experiencing mental distress vary significantly, more recently HMICFRS (2018) reviewed force annual statements as part of their *Picking up the pieces* report. They stated that of the 31 forces who reported current demand, and the 22 forces that referred to future demand, almost all reported an increase in mental health related demand. This ranged from a 40 per cent increase across the year, to 3 per cent per day (2018: 39).

Moreover, mental health demand is difficult to comprehend due to the range of incidents as a result of more immediate work often associated with mental health crisis, but also neighbourhood work which can involve mental health (HMICFRS, 2018). Police also have a key role in their localities as part of multiagency responses to mental distress, for instance through partnership meetings (Bradley, 2009) and as part of adult safeguarding. Indeed, some of the mental health demand is thought to come from other agencies directly, or as a consequence of resource issues and/or no available support for the police.

Key issues in mental health and policing

Such concerns are part of the wider ongoing issues of multiagency collaboration, especially where resources and risk are concerned. In 2012, the Independent Commission on Mental Health and Policing (Adebowale, 2013) was tasked to review the response of the MPS to those whose contact with the police, or experience in custody, had resulted in injury or death. Here, it was recognised that a collaborative approach between the police and other agencies was vital to avoid poor outcomes such as delays in accessing appropriate treatment.

The Crisis Care Concordat was launched in 2014, which recognised the need for a more coordinated approach to crisis care in particular. This report acknowledged that individuals in crisis had died due to a lack of coordination between public services and that individuals should have access to care as soon as possible. The Concordat stated that the police should be supported by health and social care agencies in order to support those in crisis at the earliest opportunity.[1] Mental health triage is one outcome of the increased policy push for partnership working between the police and agencies such as the NHS.[2] NHS Confederation, 2015), intended to facilitate interprofessional and system-level cooperation and organisation (Reveruzzi and Pilling, 2016).

However, concerns around interagency work and demand have come to the surface again more recently. In the perhaps aptly named *Picking up the pieces* report (HMICFRS, 2018), it was described that where other agencies are off duty, responsibility and risk is still passed to the police. During their encounters with those experiencing acute mental distress, frontline officers have to make crucial operational decisions based on a range of factors including the mental health of the individuals. They may or may not decide to attend an incident, they may arrest or detain an individual under section 136 of the MHA, decide no further action is required or seek mental health support for the person in need. Despite this, concerns about the amount of training officers have in relation to mental health endures.

In response to numerous calls to improve police training (Adebowale, 2013), the HMICFRS report (2018) stated that while police forces were investing in training, the quality was inconsistent. A study by Lamb and Tarpey (2019) reported that officers found their mental health training 'limited'. This suggests that there is likely to be uncertainty and inconsistency across the police force regarding their confidence, attitude towards and knowledge of mental distress. Where triage is concerned, the introduction of mental health expertise was to assist officers in decision making.[3] Decisions pertaining to section 136 of the MHA have so far been the main focus in much of the literature surrounding mental health triage and were arguably one of the main initial drivers for its implementation (Department of Health and Home Office, 2014; Durcan et al, 2014).

The inappropriate use of section 136 was located in wider concerns around individuals being taken to police cells where they were detained by officers (Her Majesty's Inspectorate of Constabulary [HMIC] et al, 2013)[4] which can breach the human rights of individuals (Morgan and Patterson, 2017). While studies do note good practice where police encounter those experiencing mental distress, most feedback points to the negative experiences of service-users (Jones and Mason, 2002; Durcan et al, 2014), including research that takes into account the introduction of the Policing and Crime Act 2017.

This act made changes to the way section 136 was implemented, including making it only acceptable to use a police cell as a place of safety in exceptional circumstances for adults, unacceptable in all circumstances for those under

18 and specified that it is necessary for officers to consult a mental health professional before detaining an individual on section 136. However research by Sondhi et al (2018) and Sondhi and Williams (2019) suggest the experiences of those who come into contact with the police could still be non-therapeutic, including for instance feelings of criminalisation. More research is needed to understand the implementation of section 136, including the impact on and experiences of individuals experiencing acute distress.

It is clear from the policy literature that it is now the status quo that the police have an ongoing role in mental health provision. However, the prevailing discourse remains that police are not experts, they are not the most appropriate agency, and nor do they necessarily know the best way to deal with a situation which may lead to poor outcomes for the individual in need (HMICFRS, 2018). Despite this, little is still known about the frontline experiences of officers who come into contact with those experiencing mental distress, and the nature of this work in the UK, which has been noted elsewhere (Marsden et al, 2020).

UK research suggests that while dealing with mental distress is perceived as a fundamental part of police work, some police can feel mental health related work is 'inappropriate' (Lane, 2019), and can be anxious to avoid blame where decisions about individuals are made (Lamb and Tarpey, 2019). McLean and Marshall (2010) reported that while officers in their study saw themselves as at times having a positive and appropriate role where mental health emergencies occur, it was also perceived that an improper level of responsibility is placed on the police due to issues in health services. Studies show that officers report difficulties with multiagency working, the limitations of police training and the value of officer experience when supporting those experiencing mental distress (McLean and Marshall, 2010; Lamb and Tarpey, 2019; Marsden et al, 2020). This chapter thus aims to build on this research by detailing the perspectives of police staff and mental health triage practitioners on the role of the police and the nature of their work where mental health is concerned.

The research study

The research presented in this chapter forms part of a project exploring the processes involved in the practice of mental health triage and the outcomes for police staff and those who come into contact with the service. The current study focused on two mental health triage teams in the north of England, both governed by the same NHS Trust and situated in the same police force, these will be referred to as site 1 and site 2 and compared throughout this chapter. Site 1 was a large rural area with small urban, often coastal centres, while site 2 was a large urban centre. Each site covered three police neighbourhoods and had a street triage team which could provide support to officers. There was also force control room phone provision which responded to officers in both sites which was integrated as part of the working team in site 2. Table 6.1 provides some brief detail as to the model components in this study.

The use of two sites allowed for a comparison of the policing and mental health triage approaches in each site. Ethnographic methods were utilised, meaning the researcher spent a lot of time with the triage teams during their day-to-day work (Brewer, 2000). The teams were observed in the office as well as when they were working with the police, and during times where individuals had a mental health assessment. Observations of the triage teams' daily work were combined with 43 semi-structured interviews. This means participants were asked predetermined open questions which they could answer and discuss with the researcher how they chose, which generated new questions. Fourteen triage team members, including mental health nurses and support workers, were interviewed. Twenty-one police staff, including inspectors, sergeants and constables, were also interviewed. These officers were sampled from the whole of the police force taking part in the research and were separate to the triage team, coming into contact with them through

Table 6.1: Site models

Model components	Triage site 1	Triage site 2
In person or phone response?	Both	Force control room triage: phone response Street triage: both
First or second responders?	Secondary response to the police as they are expected to remain at the scene until it is deemed safe they leave	Force control room triage: secondary response to police Street triage: secondary response to the police as they are expected to remain at the scene until it is deemed safe they leave
Who can request the team to respond?	Police staff and proactive response from triage	Police staff and proactive response by both teams
Eligibility criteria	All ages and any concern for mental health as perceived by the police	Both triage teams accept individuals that are 16 and above with any mental health vulnerability
Mode of transport	Dedicated triage car	Force control room triage: n/a Street triage: dedicated triage car
Types of engagement	In-person advice to police and service-users. Telephone advice to police and service users	Force control room triage: in-person advice to police staff in the control room; telephone advice to police or service users in both sites 1 and 2 Street triage: in-person advice to police and service-users. Telephone advice to police and service-users

work. Finally, eight key informants were interviewed who had come into contract with mental health triage through for instance interagency working or due to a mental health related incident.

To organise the data taken from the interviews and observations, thematic analysis was used to uncover patterns of meaning in the data (Braun and Clarke, 2006), which means that themes in the data were identified. These interviews and observations were transferred to Microsoft Word, where what the participants talked about, or what was observed, was labelled. This is known as coding and helps to understand what the data means (Coffey and Atkinson, 2006). The coding process was aided by NVivo 12, a computer program that enabled the organisation of the codes and corresponding text from the interviews and observations. This aided in organising these codes into themes in the data which was vital leading up to writing about the themes, and allowed a coherent story of the mental health triage process to be developed.

This research was very much concerned with the *whole* process of mental health triage, rather than having a specific focus on the mental health triage team encounter which tends to be the focus of research in this area. This research encouraged police and mental health triage practitioners to share their practice stories revealing the nature their work, as well as their thoughts on the purpose and how they conceptualised and implemented mental health triage. The resulting dataset provided a detailed account of the real ground-level issues and dilemmas police face when they encounter those experiencing mental distress, which will now be presented.

Findings: ground-level issues identified by the police and triage practitioners

During this study participants expressed what they felt were the specific issues that could arise when the police encountered those experiencing mental distress. This generally very much reflected policy concerns, as the issues identified by participants concerned a perceived increase in demand and the changing role of the police, interagency working, training needs and frontline dilemmas where assessment is concerned. The role of the police in mental health encounters was illuminated by participants where they discussed the changing role of police work and their attitudes towards mental health, the role of the police in protecting the public, the perceptions about the increasing demand being placed on the police to respond to mental distress and why this may be.

The changing role of the police

Another way to frame demand on the police was put forward by a Police Community Support Officer (PCSO) in site 2. They felt their increased involvement in mental health work was due to the changing nature of the role of the police:

> 'Even when I joined four and a half years ago I don't really remember dealing with mental health like we do now ... before somebody was getting stones thrown at their house, and it's the weirdo down the road; oh right, well let us know if they come back. And now it's, why are they throwing stones, who's the weirdo that lives in the house, what's going and why are they being targeted, why are they vulnerable, how can we protect them?' (Police staff)

This is interesting as this quote suggests people's behaviour is being framed differently, with a focus on the root cause. It could be that steps the police are taking, such as training to more effectively respond to the increasing demand of mental distress, is giving them more work. Certainly, officers across both sites discussed a shift in the role of policing as well as attitudes towards dealing with mental distress.

> '[P]eople, you know, were dismissive of mental health problems and things like that ... in the past they'd be probably, there's probably a culture of try and wash their hands of stuff as, as quick as you can.' (Police staff)

For practitioners and officers the culture in the police had more recently shifted to dealing with people in a less confrontational, more understanding way. A pair of officers from site 1 described how they felt the police were moving to becoming more responsible in relation to mental health issues and that the police were changing to become more supportive and respectful.

Similar views were also expressed across site 2. One practitioner felt that mental distress was being seen less negatively, where people aren't just seen as 'nutters', leading to the police thinking differently about how they deal with people with mental health issues.

> 'I think people are seeing it in less of a negative way; it's not just, oh it's another nutter. ... Yeah, kind of those concepts of people with mental health issues are changing and the way that they look at people with mental health issues has changed the; and they've actually started to think about their own mental health too.' (Triage practitioner)

This was also reflected by officers in the site, one of whom in a more supervisory role noted that with increased mental health awareness, training and the introduction of mental health initiatives, the culture has changed. This raises questions as to if changing police culture is encouraging demand.

The same officer felt like their role is much more that of a social worker and that there is more of a call for the caring side of the police, an observation that has been made about the police elsewhere (Rogers and Wintle, 2020).

Generally, the officers and practitioners across both sites welcomed the change in attitudes and emphasis on the caring role of the police. However, frustration was not absent from discussions with the police. Contrary to the officers' general positive attitudes to mental health, some accounts did reference the discontent themselves and their colleagues could feel, for instance because of old-school attitudes, resentment at the idea of others inputting into their decisions, or because mental health work was taking time away from the police involvement in crime work.

'I promised to go and visit this victim of domestic violence and stuff like that and can't go now.' (Police staff)

This suggests that victims of crime may be losing time with officers due to the time officers are spending in dealing with mental distress. The same officer felt this was unlikely to change in the future as there isn't anyone else people can call. It also appears then that while the police are perceived to be having more contact with those experiencing mental health issues, there is still some resentment that this is taking away from dealing with 'real' police work, which has also been observed elsewhere (Lane, 2019).

Similarly, another supervisory officer in site 2 described that while they try and get the right result for people, officers can be physically and mentally drained by incidents:

'[W]e're going there, usually, because it's gone horribly wrong ... and they're ill, but at the same time they're spitting, they're kicking, they're biting, they're calling you every name under the sun. So you can understand why people come away and think didn't join for that.' (Police staff)

This suggests police attitudes to this work may be related to the conditions of the work, rather than mental health per se. Similarly, another supervisory officer from the same site accepted that at times in the past, resentment at having to take responsibility for mental distress related incidents could affect how it was dealt with. However, officers across both sites regularly noted their role in the protection of people under Article 2 of the Human Rights Act, meaning by law, the police have a duty to protect individuals whose life may be at risk.

'[A]nd it's like actually if you think back to the oath you swore you've got a duty to go and preserve life and protect property and all that kind of stuff, and this actually falls within that remit.' (Police staff)

Officers often reasoned that they were duty bound where mental health was concerned, to protect and keep people safe, suggesting they may always have a role where responding to mental health is concerned.

Increasing demand on the police

Police officers across both sites overwhelmingly reported an increase in mental health related work. Officers speculated as to why this may be, which included the lack of resources of other services to meet demand, societal pressures exacerbating or causing distress for individuals such as pressure in the school systems and community breakdown, increasing public visibility, recognition and acceptability of mental health issues, and a possible increase of individuals in mental health crisis.

> '[W]hether there is more poorly people, you know, more people with mental health issues now than there used to be … there's more being brought to our attention. What the reason for that is I don't know … if we're having to deal with more and more mental health issues, we should have more and more with dealing with that, like including street triage, you know?' (Police staff)

Interagency working

Participants across both sites viewed the police service as a burden-bearing agency that would have to respond and take responsibility where mental distress was concerned. Officers' accounts revealed they found this very challenging. In site 2, one officer described that the NHS and mental health services would find it easy to 'unburden' themselves on the police.

> '[A]nd people ringing the crisis team, in crisis, and they were saying, tell you what, I think you need to ring the police. And, and we, then we were, people in mental health crisis were being directed to the police by the mental health services, which is crazy.' (Police officer)

For police in both sites, the lack of support they received from other services, as well as the limited options available to them when encountering those with mental distress, was frustrating. Officers generally ended up taking individuals to accident and emergency departments or detaining them under section 136 of the MHA where they would be taken to section 136 suite. Mental distress related work could be extremely time-consuming for officers who often came across complex dilemmas. Officers cited the poor experiences for individuals, as well as organisational/resource issues.

An officer in site 2 described a case before the introduction of triage, where they had to 'muddle through':

> 'She didn't end up getting, we didn't, we didn't arrest her and we, we kind of didn't 136 her. To be honest, we just kinda muddled through. We called her an ambulance but she was too violent to go in the ambulance so we took her to the hospital in the police vehicle, and ended up kinda sat on her all night, just restraining her until, until she calmed down and then we just left her in the care of the ambulance.' (Police staff)

In this case it appears the role of the police was entirely to restrain the individual. Where officers described doing this there was often a sense of regret, while others seemed quite detached, which may be a defence mechanism.

Organisational and resource issues were also noted, which resonates with findings from Edmondson and Cummins (2014) who reported that police felt resources of agencies were stretched and accessing support was difficult. An officer in site 2 noted that in the past there was nothing for officers before triage. Hospital was where individuals would frequently be taken but there were issues with arranging this. The following quote illustrates ongoing issues over ownership over the individual:

> 'You knew they had, you had to try and get 'em to hospital but that was nearly impossible and then there was also a massive issue, as there still is, about who's gonna transport 'em to hospital, whether it's us or an ambulance.' (Police staff)

Similarly, even where section 136 had been implemented, problems with the resources of other agencies could persist. In site 2 an officer reported that where an individual was taken to the section 136 suite after being detained, officers could find themselves waiting with the individual due to the suite not being staffed properly. In site 1, another officer divulged their dismay at services in general, suggesting that there was nobody else for those experiencing mental distress, but the police. Here it is clear that the officer could not understand why the police are repeatedly perceived to be the only agency there for individuals:

> '[T]here is this big hole that all these people are falling down and, you know, it just seems to be that nobody's thinking oh my God, what about all these people? We can't just let them keep falling or we can't let these people have no services available and rely on the police to do everything for 'em.' (Police staff)

What perhaps should also be considered here are the expectations of the police where they are less experienced at managing risk and have different thresholds for action than other services. Differing thresholds for action with regards to those involved with multiple services can be an ongoing point of contention in frontline work. Nevertheless, it seems that the police feel that while they support other services, they themselves are at times not supported when attending to those experiencing mental distress.

Individuals who come into contact with the police experiencing mental distress

Police officers and triage practitioners discussed the needs of individuals when describing their work with those perceived to be experiencing mental distress. This included differing diagnoses, for instance those with emotionally unstable personality disorder; psychosis; schizophrenia; dementia and 'cognitive decline' (note that this was a term that was used by officers in the study). Triage practitioners and police described a range of circumstances as the reason for bringing them into contact with those experiencing mental health distress. This included domestic violence; drugs and alcohol intoxication or addiction; bereavement; threats to harm themselves or others; missing persons; homelessness or tenancy issues and loneliness. Work with those with neurodiverse conditions such as autism and learning difficulties was also highlighted, and the cross-over with mental health issues.

Practitioners often reflected on the social nature of the work, despite both teams being set up as reactive crisis services. Practitioners in site 1 discussed this more so:

> '[I]t covers such a broad spectrum that there is jobs that we go to that are all social aspects, however there's other jobs that we go to where there's people who are suffering acute and enduring mental illnesses, or are physically unwell.' (Triage practitioner)

Relatedly, another practitioner in this site felt there was more of a focus on social issues in mental health triage than in other mental health services. This was thought to be due to the referral route of the police who are not mental health professionals and thus will refer social issues to the team. However they did also acknowledge that social issues and mental health issues impact on one another, so if the police are concerned, they will respond. This does perhaps suggest that the social focus of triage in this site may be partially due to what the police perceive a mental health issue to be.

Those who were seen as 'slipping through the net' were also discussed in this site. For instance where GPs may not appreciate the full extent of people's situations or because they may be off the radar of the mental health services.

'A lot of people that we've come across are just under the radar of mental health services; so often people that don't engage with community mental health teams, often people that just keep their head down and have, have never come, come to the attention ever of mental health teams.' (Triage practitioner)

Those with long and enduring conditions were also highlighted as a group that may require a response from mental health triage in site 1. This was particularly the case where PCSOs described the nature of their work and where they drew upon the expertise of triage. Where these officers were interviewed, emphasis was often put on the long-term nature of their problem-solving role in the community, rather than the short-term intervention of response work:

'So response obviously deal with the short issue and lockup ... we deal with the long term neighbour issues ... so if it somebody's, for example, someone from mental health, the chances are we will have a major contribution of work in that person cos we go there on a daily basis picking up the jobs that are reported, supporting 'em.' (Police staff)

'[B]ecause I'm trying to pick up the pieces afterwards; so, trying to understand why that incident's unfolded, why it's happened in a certain way, and mental health concern's part of that and how do we go forward from there dealing with it in the long-term future rather than just there and then.' (Police staff)

This in turn raises questions about the nature of the work the police are doing with individuals, which is often described as only pertaining to 'crisis work' in the policy literature. The longer term work highlighted in this site was perceived to pertain to where individuals had ongoing mental health needs with setbacks in their recovery; where individuals were perceived as not wanting to engage with services and also where there were perceived problems around ongoing relationships between service users and care services. Three officers described that individuals sometimes may have a blip in their recovery or a flare up as a result of long-term conditions. This was echoed by one of the triage practitioners who explained that service users coming back to the attention of the team fall into two categories, one of which was those who are generally coping, but who occasionally need more input:

'[Y]ou'll have the old-fashioned revolving door ... probably another reason why street triage are there really, because sometimes they don't need services and they cope really well but then, but then they're

not very tolerant and something happens and they go into crisis.'
(Triage practitioner)

The other group described by the same practitioner were those who were having issues with the services they were working with. When discussing repeat presenters another practitioner noted that these individuals often may not feel they are getting the answers from services that they want and will move from service to service. One officer also observed this behaviour, noting that some individuals just will not take the advice of professionals, leading to them coming to the attention of the police time and time again. Indeed, officers noted the importance of engagement, and some people's lack of willingness here. Nevertheless, some officers in this site felt mental health services were letting service-users down in the long run:

'Because a lot of the time in mental health they just get bounced, bounced around and nothing really actually gets better for them.'
(Police staff)

Similarly, two of the street triage practitioners also described their own frustrations with mental health services where individuals are discharged due to engagement issues because of being unwell, or because they have difficult lives, leading them, for instance, to forgetting they have an appointment.

'The real frustrating area for me is the people under the CMHT [community mental health team] radar that don't engage and the levels of frustration when people are discharged from community mental health teams because they don't engage, and the reason they're not engaging is because they're unwell.' (Triage practitioner)

Knowledge and training

Police training and knowledge was mentioned as a concern for officers despite some of them having supplementary mental health training. These concerns reflect the policy literature, and resonate with some research that suggests police may not be confident when dealing with mental health (Dyer et al, 2015). It should be noted that this section is not a criticism or judgement of frontline police staff, but a narrative based on the accounts of those who were involved in the triage scheme and who were asked to talk directly about the difficulties they face.

Questions as to the level at which the police should be operating as mental health professionals came up regularly as a point of debate during observations of practice with the triage practitioners and during some interviews. Some practitioners were sympathetic to the complex dilemmas the police faced on the front line.

'[Because] actually some of the incidents that they have to attend are completely out of their knowledge and experience, and understandably so.' (Triage practitioner)

During interviews, participants across both sites felt that officers were not adequately equipped to deal with those with whom they came into contact who experienced mental distress due to their training and knowledge. One officer noted that before the introduction of street triage and the mental health training, they reacted to mental distress related incidents as a member of the public might, citing that their training was criminal justice focused:

'As police officers, you know, we're expected to be police officers, paramedics to a certain extent, mental health workers, social workers, housing officers, basically we're expected to be everything; however, we are trained in the law.' (Police staff)

Relatedly, another officer described that while they had had some training, they didn't feel they were anywhere near the level of a mental health worker, or ambulance staff. Concerns were also raised by participants about the adequacy of the police and the specifics of different mental illnesses. One participant reported that no matter how much training frontline officers were given, they didn't feel that the police were ever an appropriate response to mental distress

There was also some discussion among officers about the police approach to those experiencing mental distress. One officer felt that while they may try their best, police can struggle to talk to people. It can be hard to strike a balance between saying the wrong thing and 'mollycoddling' individuals. Another officer felt that mental distress related incidents were generally guesswork. They described that the police often made the problem worse by not knowing what to say, or not understanding the individual. Indeed, interviews presented the police approach to be characterised by efficiency and a desire to problem-solve.

'[S]ometimes our way of dealing with people is quite assertive. "What are you doing, why are you doing it and what can we do to sort it?"' (Police staff)

In contrast to this, however, one practitioner acknowledged the skills of the police especially in relation to communication, but also felt their knowledge wasn't specific enough for the encounters they faced. Throughout observations of practice, practitioners regularly acknowledged how skilled the police could be. However, even where officers felt they were experienced, there was still an acknowledged need:

'Whereas yes we've all had mental health experience in dealing with police incidents but it's not, it's not specialised in any way shape or form. It's not a qualification or an actual level of experience at dealing and resolving situations of a mental health nature.' (Police staff)

It is then is no surprise that officers who perceive an increase in mental distress related incidents and to which they are not trained to respond, struggled with making difficult decisions where dilemmas arose in frontline practice.

Assessment, decisions and dilemmas

The interviews illuminated some of the complex frontline dilemmas and decisions the police encountered, which is rarely *detailed* in the policy or research literature. Before the introduction of triage, individuals appeared to be treated like criminals when they came into contact with the police. They could end up for instance in a police van, being taken into custody, as this was the only way to be assessed. Officers across both sites described that when it came to mental distress related incidents, they often didn't know what the best of course of action was. Indeed, an officer in site 1 felt that one of the objectives of street triage was to advise them on what the course of action should be.

Risk was the main point of concern and was frequently brought up by participants during observation and interviews. It was something the police had struggled with, especially when balanced with their responsibility to the public, as previously documented in relation to Article 2 of the Human Rights Act. This also resonates with observations made in the section about interagency work, where it was suggested that police thresholds for risk are likely to be lower than those of mental health professionals due to their training.

For some officers across both sites, dealing with mental distress was scary, as well as risky. One officer in a supervisory position explained that officers fear the death of individuals. Similarly, the discomfort officers could sometimes feel in leaving individuals was described by two officers in more supervisory roles in site 1. For instance, where someone was self-harming, it was described as a big decision to make due to what is at stake.

'But even if this person's said they're gonna kill themselves ten days in a row and never do it, you're still doing that situation. You can't, as an officer, sit there, cos you're not mental health trained. No matter what they say you can't say, oh hang on a minute, you know, he's done it ten days in a row, you're gonna do, because what happens if that day's the day he goes and kills himself? It, that's, that's then on you.' (Police staff)

Here it appears the officer will not leave the fate of the individual down to chance, as the responsibility will fall back on them. Similar themes about responsibility emerged where officers described situations where what was described as 'attention-seeking' behaviour was suspected, and where there was a threat of self-harm, or if the officer didn't know if they could leave.

During interviews and observations, participants were generally empathic towards those experiencing mental distress. However, this was not always the case where 'attention-seeking' behaviours were discussed by police as part of their response to mental distress. This label was referred to where repeat callers, presenters, and where there were questions over 'genuine' need for mental health support were discussed.

'[Y]ou shouldn't say it, but often sort of you think is there just, they're, they're doing it for attention or they're doing it for the drunk or they've done it cos they've fallen out with their boyfriend or girlfriend and things like that, and, you know, it's, it's hard because sometimes you don't know what, what that person is, whether they're actually seriously going to do something.' (Police staff)

Clearly officers feel a sense of responsibility to the individuals and are unlikely to take a chance over their wellbeing, even where they suspect there may not be a perceived genuine need. As has been illustrated, officers can struggle to make decisions about the best course of action where mental distress is a factor in their work and can find such situations risky. This was particularly the case where individuals may be a risk to themselves and questions over if there was a perceived genuine mental health need. Similar difficulties also arose where questions over the implementation of section 136 played out.

The use of section 136 was regularly cited by officers and practitioners in both sites as a point of contention, with practitioner interviews suggesting there was a perception that they could still be overused or inappropriately implemented as is reflected in the policy literature. Officers in both sites described that they often felt the use of section 136 was their only option, was used out of convenience or where there they deemed the situation risky.

'Police officers and staff were hoping that something would reach a level of mental health where that person didn't have capacity and therefore we could 136 them, or an ambulance would come ... we're all deep down selfish people and we all wanna cover our own backs, we obviously want to look after that person ... but we also don't want to be the last person to see that person and we haven't given them the service that they need because there isn't one.' (Police staff)

It is important to consider here the notion of the use of section 136 as 'inappropriate', which is often oversimplified in the policy literature, as for the police it may be necessary if there isn't another option for them, regardless of the level of need of the individual experiencing mental distress. Indeed, one triage practitioner felt that section 136 was a means of officers controlling the situation without further escalating it.

However, such debates are also made more complicated where the implementation of the act is dubious, and where the service-user's experience is made more unpleasant. Interestingly, a couple of officers acknowledged the historical uses of section 136 may not have been entirely appropriate where individuals were 'persuaded' to come into a public setting from a private setting, often their home. Similarly, for one officer the use of force with individuals was also seen as a negative consequence of police involvement where section 136 was concerned:

'Last time I was at hospital with a, with someone who'd been 136'd, he spent all night in handcuffs because he was violent to start with. ... So then when the psychiatrist came afterwards and he was like "Oh why, why have you handcuffed him? This is ridiculous, you know, you're not, you're making things worse".' (Police staff)

These considerations are important as they may compound the individual's distress. Similar issues were discussed in relation to where individuals could be arrested or criminalised. One officer described a historical scenario where they felt that if triage had been available to them, the outcome would have been different:

'I ended up having to deploy pepper spray. Ehm which gave us enough distraction to control the situation, and we detained him on a, not sure what we detained him on. Think it was a breach of the peace, because there was a risk of his own safety to himself. So that's how that, had that situation been seven or eight years in the future, that situation would have been completely different.' (Police staff)

The same officer registered their resentment at having to use force against individuals and lock them up knowing that they were in crisis. Indeed, the final dilemma that was raised by participants centred around the decision to arrest or prosecute, which could be a potential outcome for those experiencing mental distress. However, contrary to that which one may expect, this often related to the fear officers had of arresting individuals who they perceived to be experiencing mental distress. This was a recurrent issue highlighted in both interviews and observations of practice.

Participants across both sites described that the police were scared to arrest people, and as a result, perceived that some individuals didn't face the consequences of their behavior:

> '[W]e have a lot of service users who commit regular offences and get absolutely nothing, nothing for it.' (Triage practitioner)

This is perhaps surprising, especially when recognised by triage practitioners as inappropriate, as they are there to be an advocate for the service-user. However there was discussion among some practitioners during observations of practice around the stigma of assuming those experiencing mental distress can't take responsibility for their actions.

As has been shown, police feel that they are not best placed to deal with mental distress and are often the service of last resort to do so. Despite the perceived increasing and changing role of officers in dealing with those who may have complex and enduring needs, officers still feel they lack knowledge and training with respect to those experiencing mental distress. Participants across both sites described difficulties where police had to determine the needs of individuals and then had to make decisions about the 'best' course of action.

Conclusion

Participants in this study described ongoing issues with increasing mental health related demand and perceived their roles as situated in the wider context of societal pressures, service resource issues, as well as the public's awareness of mental health and increasing levels of mental distress. However, the data also illuminated perceptions around the changing culture of the police, which was thought to be more supportive of those experiencing mental distress. There was also discussion among participants about the involvement of the police in looking at the causes and circumstances around mental distress, especially in the case of the longer-term work mentioned by the PCSOs.

This is somewhat a departure from the focus on mental health 'crisis' usually at the heart of discussions around police responses to those experiencing mental distress. It also raises questions as to if the nature of the demand being placed on the police is changing how they respond, and perhaps if the police are consequently creating demand due to the changing culture and their role where mental health is concerned? It has been observed that as a consequence of the introduction of mental health triage, individuals in crisis may ring the police to access a mental health service as they are the only option (HMICFRS, 2018).

This in turn raises further questions around responsibility for those experiencing mental distress and where the police service should fit into this. The National Police Chiefs Council (2020) National Strategy on Policing and Mental Health describes the police's role in keeping individuals experiencing mental distress safe where absolutely necessary because of a threat to public safety or to an individual's life. However, as this chapter has shown the police role in responding to mental distress may be evolving to cope with the perceived increasing demand and complex work they encounter. There arguably remains a lack of understanding and consequently clarity around the role of the police where mental health is concerned, compounded by our lack of understanding around the nature of demand, which has been observed elsewhere (Williams et al, 2020).

It is important to stress here that wider systems can't be ignored. Issues around mental health and policing can't and shouldn't be seen as separate from concerns around the wider mental health system. As was evident in the responses from participants, and reflecting the policy concerns already discussed, the police can feel as if they are taking responsibility from other services and plugging gaps. Austerity measures introduced in 2010 are relevant here, which have seen the retrenchment and reform of the welfare state in the UK, the effects of which are likely to endure (Edmiston, 2018). Due to funding cuts, mental health services may not have adequate resources to care for individuals who reside in the community. This in turn has led to demand on the police to help respond to mental distress in the community (Cummins, 2018b, 2020a). While more money has been promised for mental health provision, this is unlikely to meet the demands needed to sustain or improve services (Trades Union Congress, 2018).

Taking this into account, McDaniel (2019) is arguably more frank about the reality of the role of the police and their discretion where working with those experiencing mental distress, and places emphasis on the need for the 'policing organisation' to become more treatment led, to promote 'an ethos of accountability, transparency and ethics' (2019: 90). The position taken here is that it is important that mental health remains on the police agenda as it does appear in the current socio-economic and political context of the UK that the police will continue to play a large role in mental health. At the heart of these encounters are individuals in distress who deserve to be treat with compassion, dignity and respect.

Kane (2020) offers some insight into how we may practically move forward, by promoting transferable lessons from the US CIT model evidence base emphasising better local service integration, local leadership, information sharing and staff training (for both police and health staff who come across numerous dilemmas). As such, the continued roll out of training as recommended by HMICFRS (2018) and the National Police Chiefs Council (2020) will be vital for officers moving forward. Moreover, our understanding and evaluation of mental health triage must continue (HMICFRS, 2018; National Police Chiefs Council, 2020) in order to understand its effectiveness. At present little is still known about the outcomes, particularly the long-term outcomes of mental health triage, the practice dilemmas faced at the interface of the mental health and criminal justice system as well as service-user experiences here. It is ethically imperative to ensure these schemes are better understood given their widespread implementation across England and Wales, the urgency of which seems to have tailed off in recent years.

Nevertheless, questions around the *ultimate responsibility* and acceptability of police involvement endure. The continuing role of, and arguable appropriation of, the police in responding to mental distress must be always be scrutinised where concerns endure over their continued involvement, which at worst can lead to the death of individuals experiencing mental distress (Baker and Pillinger, 2020). As noted by Morgan and Patterson (2017), where the police are seen as the primary response to mental health crisis, there will always be the potential for breaches of the human rights of the individual at the centre of the contact. Indeed, Vitale (2017) argues the issues here are more fundamental and will not be resolved by police reform due to the incompatibility of police authority with empowerment and protection, which don't themselves always sit well together. As noted by Cummins (2020b), this sentiment is echoed in service-user and policing groups.

Further reading

Cummins, I. and Edmondson, D. (2016) Policing and street triage. *Journal of Adult Protection*, 18(1), 40–52.

Marsden, M., Nigam, J., Lemetyinen, H. and Edge, D. (2020) Investigating police officers' perceptions of their role in pathways to mental healthcare. *Health & Social Care in the Community*, 28(3), 913–921.

Reveruzzi, B. and Pilling S. (2016) *Street triage: report on the evaluation of nine pilot schemes in England*. Available at: https://s16878.pcdn.co/wp-content/uploads/2016/09/Street-Triage-Evaluation-Final-Report.pdf

Riley, G., Freeman, E., Laidlaw, J. and Pugh, D. (2011) A frightening experience: detainees' and carers' experiences of being detained under Section 136 of the Mental Health Act. *Medicine, Science and the Law*, 51(3), 164–169.

Rogers, C. and Wintle, E. (2020) Accessing justice for mental health sufferers? A comparison of UK and Australian developments. In J.L.M. McDaniel, K. Moss and K.G. Pease (eds) *Policing and mental health: theory policy and practice*. Abingdon: Routledge.

Shapiro, G.K., Cusi, A., Kirst, M., O'Campo, P., Nakhost, A. and Stergiopoulos, V. (2015) Co-responding police-mental health programs: a review. *Administration and Policy in Mental Health and Mental Health Services Research*, 42(5), 606–620.

Sondhi, A. and Williams, E. (2019) Police and health operational staff perspectives on managing detainees held under Section 136 of the Mental Health Act: a qualitative study in London. *Journal of Community Safety and Well-Being*, 4(4), 88–93.

Sondhi, A., Luger, L., Toleikyte, L. and Williams, E. (2018) Patient perspectives of being detained under Section 136 of the Mental Health Act: findings from a qualitative study in London. *Medicine, Science and the Law*, 58(3), 159–167.

7

Defunding the police: a mental health perspective

Introduction

This chapter considers how the calls to 'defund the police' might impact on police mental health work. The 'defund the police' movement developed as part of the Black Lives Matter (BLM) movement. The wider BLM movement has its origins in protests against police violence, brutality and the systemic racism that underpins it. BLM seeks to overturn these long-standing racial and social injustices. Policing and police violence are a key factor in the maintenance of racial hierarchies and the suppression of Black political movements for political justice and full citizenship (Hinton, 2021). In the US context, 'defund the police' argues that the policing cannot be reformed – a radical change is required. For example, Purnell (2021) calls for the abolition of the police as part of a radical programme of social reform. Reformist positions have been argued for a shift in funding from policing towards an investment in welfare and community services. In calling for this policy shift, campaigners have highlighted the need for significant investment in mental health services.

As we have seen in earlier chapters, the police role in mental health services increased because of the failings of community care. The result is that people with mental health problems have increasing been drawn into the CJS, which has become a default provider of mental health care. This is clearly a role that, despite the best efforts of staff, the CJS is not equipped to perform. For the police, this has meant that officers have increasingly become first responders in situations where individuals are experiencing mental health crises. This chapter outlines the development of the call to 'defund the police'. It suggests that, if we move beyond the confrontational rhetoric of its opponents, we can see that 'defund the police' is call for a programme of social investment. It is, therefore, an approach that has the potential to tackle long-standing areas of concern. Service-user groups and mental health professionals highlight that police involvement in mental health emergencies is inevitably stigmatising.

There is a wide recognition that mental health services are failing to provide appropriate responses to those in crisis (Wessley, 2018). As well as being an issue of human rights and social justice, these failures place vulnerable people at increased risk. Police involvement in mental health work has grown because of austerity and the wider retrenchment in public services. Police officers on an organisational and individual level feel that they are often left 'picking up the pieces' (HMICFRS, 2018). 'Defund the police' can actually be attractive to police officers as an approach. An increase in and new forms of mental health crisis services that will, in theory, reduce the level of police mental health work or provide more support for officers.

Black Lives Matter

BLM began in the US but has spread across the world. The origins of BLM can be found in the community response to the acquittal of George Zimmerman in the summer of 2013. Zimmerman had shot 17-year-old African-American Trayvon Martin in Florida 2012. The case highlighted the issue of racial profiling as well as Florida's 'stand your ground laws'. The gay founders of BLM, Patrisse Khan-Cullors, Opal Tometi and Alicia Garza, based the movement on a broader intersectional analysis that focuses on gender and sexual freedom alongside attacking racial injustice (Green and Tong, 2019). BLM became a movement that campaigned for wider racial and economic social justice. It gathered momentum following a series of deaths of African-Americans involving contact with the police. For example, the shooting of Michael Brown, an 18-year-old high school student in Ferguson, Missouri led to a series of protests. These events are not new in the US. However, the emergence of smart phones and social media mean that there is now video evidence to demonstrate that the police use of force has been completely disproportionate and underpinned by deeply engrained stereotypes of Black masculinity and alleged criminality. In 2020, the murder of George Floyd in Minneapolis led to calls to 'defund the police'. These calls were based on the argument that an increasingly militarised police force (Harcourt, 2018) was being called upon to police or respond to problems that were, at their root, the problems of poverty (Vitale, 2017). These are social issues that the police are not necessarily equipped or trained to deal with. The increased use of imprisonment and the wider involvement of police as the first response to a whole range of social issues has been a significant feature of neoliberalism (Cummins, 2020c).

The expansion of the US penal state has impacted disproportionately on poor, urban African-American communities (Wacquant, 2002; Drucker, 2011; Alexander, 2012). It is not possible to simply to argue that the UK or other countries are following a similar module as the US penal state (Cummins, 2019). It is vital that the historical, political, economic and social factors that have created the current situation are acknowledged. However, there are some parallels between the situation in the US and UK. The Lammy Review (2017) highlighted the continue overrepresentation of people from BAME backgrounds in the CJS in England and Wales. One of the key areas that BLM and 'defund the police' have highlighted is the police role in mental health work. The US police budgets have increased in a period in which crime has been falling. Since the 1970s, spending on police has nearly tripled, reaching US$114.5 billion in 2017 (Bliss, 2020). 'Defund the police' has been caricatured by its opponents as aiming to disband the police entirely. As in any social movement, there is a range of opinion. Vitale (2017) argues that the police are poorly trained and ill-equipped to perform these 'social work roles'. This is partly due to what Vitale (2017) called the 'warrior' mindset of modern urban policing. The result is that there is a danger that difficult and tense situations lead to conflict on both an individual and societal level. The excessive use of force and the escalation of essentially minor incidents can lead to fatalities. George Floyd died after the police were called when a shopkeeper was suspicious that he used a counterfeit dollar bill. These are individual and family tragedies. They undermine wider societal confidence in the police, which is fragile or lacking in the communities that actually need protection most in the US (Baker and Pillinger, 2019; Campbell, 2019; Sherman, 2020) and Australia (Thomas, 2020). Shapiro et al (2015) initiatives in policing and mental health have come about because of fatalities following police contacts with individuals experiencing a mental health crisis. Such cases are vitally important. However, they do not capture the totality of police involvement in mental health work. Wood et al (2017) concluded that the majority of mental health calls do not involve violence or reach a threshold where compulsory admission to hospital would be required. The majority of calls fall into what they term the 'gray zone' of police work.

What is the police role in mental health?

This is the fundamental question that this volume seeks to answer.

The police welfare role is not limited to the field of mental health. The majority of modern policing is concerned with these issues. Police mental health work has to be placed in this context. There is a danger of 'othering' people with mental health problems here – assuming that police officers only come into contact with people when they are in crisis. This is simply not the case. Police officers encounter people with mental health problems in all areas of their work. They are colleagues, fellow professionals, victims of crime and so on. In Chapter 5, we examined the mental health of officers and the increased recognition that the role and its demands can have a detrimental impact on individuals. Police involvement in mental health work has to be viewed as part of their role in wider community safety and the protection of vulnerable people. One feature of modern policing has been the way that on an individual and organisational level it has become involved in a increasing series of roles. As we have seen, there is an ongoing debate how appropriate these roles, particularly in mental health, actually are.

These tasks are additional to the traditional function of the maintenance of law and order and the apprehension of offenders. Austerity policies in the UK saw police forces struggling to meet increased demand with reduced resources (Walley and Adams, 2019). In the 2019 General Election, the Tories announced that they would aim to recruit 20,000 new officers. As a number of commentators pointed out, this would restore police numbers to their 2010 level. The increased demands on the police are not simply the result of austerity and reduced police numbers. These are clearly important. It is important to highlight other factors that impact on the use of police resources. These include changes in the nature of offences, such as the rise in digital crime, the increase in sexual offences and population changes. Finally, the police role in the response to the COVID-19 pandemic has clearly required a shift in resources. All these factors combine to shape the police role and resource demand in complex ways (Laufs et al, 2020). Alongside this broad national picture, it is important to look at the way that these factors play out at a force, divisional and neighbourhood level.

One of the most complex and challenging areas is the police involvement in mental health work. Police officers often act as first responders, in situations where people are experiencing severe mental health episodes. If family, carers or members of the public are concerned that an individual's extreme or unpredictable behavior is posing a danger to themselves and members of the public then they are likely to make a 999 call to the police. There have been a range of initiatives such as mental health triage to try and tackle these issues. It is widely recognised that closer working between the police and mental health agencies can ensure that individuals receive timely and appropriate mental health interventions (Rodgers et al, 2019). Increased police involvement is the result of the failures of community care and the long-term underinvestment in mental health services (Rogers and Wintle, 2020). Similar trends are visible across Europe, Australia and New Zealand, and North America (Cummins, 2020a). These trends have strengthened over the past ten years but they have deeper roots. In the first wave of deinstitutionalisation, Bittner (1967, 1970) identified that police beat officers were increasingly responding to those experiencing mental health difficulties. Following that work, Teplin's research (1984) confirmed this. In the UK, the role of the police was further highlighted in several community care inquiries in the 1990s – most notably the Ritchie Inquiry (Ritchie et al, 1994) into the care and treatment of Christopher Clunis. Clunis murdered Jonathan Zito at a tube station in 1992. Clunis had contact with the police and a range of other agencies following a series of compulsory admissions under the MHA. The inquiry was critical of the police response as well as highlighting the lack of interdisciplinary working (Cummins, 2012).

One of the key aims of this volume has been to examine the way that the police role in mental health has expanded. This expansion has largely been by default – I have not been able to find any calls from the police that they should take on a wider role in mental health work. The reverse is largely the case with police officers often feeling overwhelmed and frustrated by their role in mental health work. These demands lead to many officers asking fundamental questions about whether they should have any mental health role at all (Marsden et al, 2020). The official and organisational response to these questions has been a series of initiatives, such as street triage or liaison and diversion schemes that have been examined in this volume. There is a wide variety of local initiatives and different organisational structures. The fundamental aim is to improve joint working and so that individuals in crisis receive appropriate access to mental health care. These are clearly laudable aims. However, Williams et al (2020) question whether policy in this area is sufficiently clear as to what problems are being addressed and what the role of the police should be. Williams et al (2020) argue that an unintended consequence of such initiatives is that the police become more, not less, involved in mental health work. If officers do not receive appropriate training for this work, there is a danger that decision making and the exercise of police discretion are not based on sound professional knowledge and practice. The outcome is the poor provision of treatment for people with mental health problems, which also raises questions of police legitimacy (McDaniel, 2019).

Debates about the nature and extent of the police role in mental health related work have gradually become more prominent. One of the impacts of austerity has been to bring them into sharper focus. Austerity reduced mental health service provision but also increased demand (Cummins, 2018a). The emergency role of the police means that the public will seek their assistance – everyone knows that dialling 999 will produce a response. In addition, police officers are increasingly frustrated by the number of referrals that they receive from other organisations.

There are two key elements in the current debates about the police role. The first is a fundamental questioning of whether the police should have a role in mental health related work. The second is a concern that police are being asked to take on an increasing role in mental health related work. The Bradley Review (2009) and the Home Affairs Select Committee Report in 2015 both highlighted concerns about the police role in this area. In October 2018, the House of Commons Home Affairs Committee published a report, *Policing for the future*. Dee Collins, Chief Constable of West Yorkshire Police, in giving evidence stated that '83% of my time in terms of delivering services is not about crime'. The report includes a focus on issues relating to vulnerable people – including people with mental health problems. Chief Constable Collins identified three areas: mental health work; missing people (particularly missing children); and multiagency child protection work. The inquiry concluded that:

A prominent theme emerging throughout this inquiry was the increasing volume of police work arising from identifying and managing various forms of vulnerability, including safeguarding vulnerable adults who cross their path, being first-on-scene during a mental health crisis, undertaking child protection work on a multi-agency basis, and dealing with repeat missing person incidents, including looked-after children.

These issues were further highlighted by the HMICFRS report (2018) *Picking up the pieces*. From its title onwards, the main thrust of the report is clear: the police are called upon to respond to too many people experiencing mental health crisis. This is not considered an appropriate use of police resources. The report repeats the long-standing concern that officers are not being appropriately trained to support people in the midst of a mental health crisis. The report goes on to argue that the organisation of services and lack of training may also put people who are experiencing a crisis at greater risk. There are several potential risks including that individuals may not receive appropriate treatment. Mental health concerns may not be identified by officers so that individuals are taken into custody, which is a further risk in itself. Police officers develop a range of skills in working in crisis situations and responding to emergencies. These are transferable to mental health work. However, this is not quite the same as feeling properly trained and supported to respond – an issue highlighted by officers themselves (Marsden et al, 2020). The report also raises the ethical question of police involvement. It is inevitably further stigmatising. This is not the intention of police involvement but, ultimately, it criminalises people who are experiencing a mental health crisis. This is an important area but only one aspect of policing and mental health. People with mental health problems are more likely than other groups to be victims of crime (Koskela et al, 2016). There are many areas of police work that are related to broader mental health issues. 'Missing persons' are one of the key areas driving increased demands on the police. Such calls are often mental health related (Parr and Stevenson, 2013). The question of getting a clear and consistent picture of police demand that is related to mental health is a difficult one. Edmondson and Cummins (2014) noted that 'mental health' was a flexible term covering a wide range of situations.

In 2013, as the fall in police numbers was being keenly felt, the then Home Secretary, Theresa May, told the police that their role 'was to cut crime no more no less'. In 2016, the former Met Commissioner, Sir Ian Blair, suggested that responding to vulnerable people in crisis was preventing the police fulfilling its core function of ensuring community safety. In 2017, Sir Tom Winsor stated the police had become the service of first not last resort for people in crisis. The HMICFRS found that, based on data obtained from 22 forces, 3 per cent of all calls were flagged as mental health. This work illustrates the concerns that police officers have about the role that they were being asked to perform. There were 318,000 incidents, around two-thirds of these calls were related to a 'concern for safety' for an individual. This is a very broad category. It may be an immediate emergency, for example, if a family member has received a text or message indicating that the person is considering harming themselves or has gone missing. However, this report indicated that 10 per cent of these concerns for safety calls came from other agencies. This is a particular source of frustration for police officers, who not without reason, feel that they are being called upon to cover for the gaps in other mental health services. This is, of course, an organisational rather than a personal issue. The report emphasised that the peak time for calls to police for support with mental health related incidents is 3pm to 6pm, Monday to Friday. The period when community services are likely to be less available. This is not to suggest that there will never be calls where it is appropriate to call the police. The police have skills and resources that other agencies lack – for example knowing how to approach looking for someone who has been reported missing. The concern from a police perspective is that officers are being asked to undertake work that is more appropriate for staff from social welfare agencies. Mental health issues are complex and often the police are being asked to respond to situations as emergencies, which are actually the result of long-term complex issues and cannot be resolved quickly. The report, for example, highlights that the five most frequent callers to the MPS made over 8,600 calls in 2017 – an average of roughly 4.5 calls every day. The HMICFRS does identify one perhaps surprising outcome of the increased role for the police in mental health work: 'One of the positive, perhaps unintended, outcomes of the police working closely with mental health professionals is that stress and wellbeing are discussed more openly, not just in terms of looking after the public but also looking after each other.'

Section 136 of the Mental Health Act

A radical approach to 'defunding the police' would have to address the gap that any abolition of sections 135 and 136 of the MHA would create. Section 136 is generally used in circumstances where a person is considered to be putting themselves or possibly others at immediate serious risk. There is no need for a formal medical diagnosis so the application of section 136 of the MHA is dependent on several factors including the experience and skills of the officer, the information they may have and the nature of the incident. The place of safety should normally be a hospital based setting. Most mental health trusts have created specially designated areas – section 136 suites – where the formal assessments can take place.

The aim of section 136 of the MHA is to ensure that a person is assessed by mental health professionals and not drawn further into the CJS. The use of police cells criminalises people experiencing a mental health crisis. The experience – however well the police respond – is bound to be a custodial rather than therapeutic one. In addition, police cells are simply not designed for this purpose. A cell is a bare concrete space with a mattress and a steel toilet. Police custody is a pressurised, busy and often chaotic environment. There is clearly the potential for this to have a negative impact on an individual's mental health. The HMIC (2013) review notes that the process is essentially the same as being arrested. From a service-user's perspective the experience was a custodial not a therapeutic one. Service-users felt that they had been criminalised, dehumanised and their dignity and human rights abused (Riley et al, 2011). The Angiolini Review (2017) reported a welcome fall in the use of police cells as places of safety. The current configuration of mental health services in England and Wales would make it impossible to abolish the police's section 136 powers – this would mean that the police would have no means of compulsory intervention other than arrest. A 'defund the police' approach, alongside a greater investment generally in community mental health services, would argue for the development of crisis centres that could be used as alternatives to hospital admission or in circumstances where the police now use section 136.

Police officers' attitudes to mental health work

Lane (2019) carried out a study of posts by police officers on an online forum, to examine attitudes to police mental health work. This research identified two clear themes in the posts. The first was the idea that responding to such incidents was effectively diverting the officers and valuable police resources from their real job of fighting crime (Lane, 2019). There was sub-theme here that constructed the callers as 'spongers', exploiting the benefits system and undeserving of a sympathetic responses. The other theme that Lane (2019) identified was one that associated mental health problems with violence. Loader (2013) argues that the police have a key role in defining the nature and extent of social problems. The powerful narrative framing of police mental health work at both the organisational and individual level is that the police are being asked to do the work of mental health agencies or cover for the inadequacies of these agencies. Despite the fact that deinstitutionalisation as a policy is now almost 60 years old, it still features in the narrative of increased pressures on the police (Frederick et al, 2018). This is an important historical factor but it can obscure the reality of more recent service retrenchment as the result of austerity (Cummins, 2018b). This narrative, like many others in mental health, marginalises the experiences of service-users. There is a danger of assuming that the police cannot respond to those experiencing a mental health crisis. This is not to suggest that police can or should be mental health professionals. It is, rather, a recognition that police officers have skills and experience in responding to citizens in some form of crisis.

The traditional response model of policing does not meet the organisational needs of the police. In addition, there is significant evidence that police encounters with people in mental health crisis carry the potential for harsher treatment of individuals, even the use of lethal force. As a result, police forces across the world have developed new models. These models have been developed as a result of national and local circumstances – often in response to a critical incident or a fatality.

Conclusion

The police have become a de facto mental health emergency care service. The progressive supporters of deinstitutionalisation argued for the money that was being spent in asylums to be diverted into well-resourced community mental health services (Cummins, 2020a). An increased role for the police was not part of these plans. Since the mid-1960s, there have been a series of concerns that the police are being drawn into mental health work – particularly responding to people in crisis. Individual officers feel that 'this is not part of the job' (Lurigio and Watson, 2010). Senior managers see the increased demands on police time and resources as unsustainable. The policy solution has been to adopt new models of working such as street triage. These models still involve police officers. There are a number of models but what they have in common are attempts to limit police involvement and ensure that citizens can access appropriate mental health care in a timely manner. The issue of the stigmatising nature of police involvement remains. One significant concern is that these models do not address the fundamental question of police involvement. The result of such models is not to reduce the police role in mental health work. One unintended consequence of such developments is that the police may become more deeply embedded in mental health work. Alongside these organisational issues, there is a wider concern that police are plastering over the deep cracks in community mental health services.

Calls to 'defund the police' began in the US, which is clearly a very different policing environment to the UK. This does not mean that it does not have lessons for this country. In many policy areas, the UK has followed US trends. US 'defund the police' calls have focused on the militarisation of the police and the impact that this has on police and community relations. The 'defund the police' movement highlights that the police budgets have been protected while other public and welfare services have been reduced. 'Defund the police' is not necessarily an abolitionist movement – this is clearly one strand of it. In the mental health sphere, it can be viewed as an extension of the progressive arguments for community care. Current mental health services have failed to achieve the ambitious goals of deinstitutionalisation. One result is the current involvement of the police in mental health work. It is clear that there needs to be greater investment in a range of mental health services. The focus on police involvement in emergency and crisis work should not obscure this. The current debates have been focused on minimising police involvement or making the response more effective. This includes the more effective use of police resources. However, the broader aim is to ensure that in emergency situations in particular, individuals receive appropriate care as soon as possible in a way that ensures their dignity and wider human rights are respected. This chapter has traced the ways that concerns about the police role in mental health work has increased over the past 20 years. These have been present in one form or another since the first wave of deinstitutionalisation in the 1960s. The recent increase in concerns has been driven by the double impact of austerity policies. In the UK, the police, unusually under a Conservative government, have not been immune to these reductions in spending. The increase in demand creates a situation where the police feel that they are 'picking up the pieces' – plastering over the gaps in mental health community services. These trends can be observed across North America, Europe and Australia and New Zealand. While there is a recognition that police involvement in mental health is, at the moment, unavoidable and something of a necessary evil, there are calls for a root and branch reform. In the mental health sphere, the calls to 'defund the police', if we take this to mean reduce police involvement, are largely supported by the police. 'Defund the police' would become part of a wider social investment that seeks to reinvigorate the progressive values that were at the heart of community care.

Further reading

Cummins, I. (2020) *Defunding the police: a mental health perspective.* Transforming Society. Available at: http://www.transformingsociety.co.uk/2020/08/17/defunding-the-police-a-mental-health-perspective/

MIND (2015) *At risk yet dismissed.* Available at: https://www.mind.org.uk/media-a/4121/at-risk-yet-dismissed-report.pdf

MIND (2020) *The mental health emergency.* Available at: https://www.mind.org.uk/media-a/5929/the-mental-health-emergency_a4_final.pdf

Thomas, S.D. (2020) Critical essay: fatal encounters involving people experiencing mental illness. *Salus Journal*, 8(2), 100.

Vitale, A.S. (2017) *The end of policing.* London: Verso.

Wood, J., Swanson, J., Burris, J.D. and Gilbert, A. (2011) *Police interventions with persons affected by mental illnesses: a critical review of global thinking.* New York: Rutgers University, Center for Behavioral Health Services and Criminal Justice Research.

Conclusion

Within the organisational culture of policing, there is the potential for mental health work to be seen as 'not proper policing'. The image of policing in the media and popular culture is very much dominated by responses to serious and violent crime. There is a danger that mental health work will be seen as having a lower status and organisational priority. Responding to a mental health emergency or other situations involving a vulnerable adult requires a different set of skills to other aspects of police work. However, there are core skills that police officers use – critical thinking, communication skills, information gathering, negotiation and decision making. Police mental health work includes a range of complex situations which are not easily resolved. Police interventions will not address the root causes of mental distress. This is a source of particular frustration for officers, who are often outcome focused (Reiner, 1992b). The most complex mental health related work is not going to be 'solved' by police intervention. Such an intervention will deal, however imperfectly, with an immediate crisis. Long-standing complex issues require long-term solutions. This is at the heart of the frustration that many police officers feel in this area of their work. One of the frustrations for officers is that they are often called to the same address on numerous occasions (Cummins and Edmondson, 2016). The HMICFRS (2018) report also highlighted the demand on police resources that repeated callers can create. This is not limited to the police response to mental health crises.

The chapters of this volume have considered the key areas of police mental health work. This role raises a number of key ethical and practice issues. On reflection, the fundamental question at the root of all these issues is 'what role, if any, should the police have in mental health work services'? The answer in this volume is a pragmatic one. The current structure of mental health services in the four countries of the United Kingdom means that it is inevitable that police officers will be involved in responding to people in mental health crisis. It is also vitally important that all aspects of police work involve contact with people experiencing mental health problems. People with mental health problems are first and foremost citizens who should be treated with dignity and respect. They are also family members, carers and work colleagues. Having acknowledged that core value perspective, if we accept that police officers will be involved in mental health work, we should seek to limit their role as far as is possible. Following on from this, we need to consider how we can create a working culture that recognises the potential psychological impacts of police work and provides appropriate advice and support.

The question of what should be the appropriate role for the police in mental health work is not a new one. As we have seen, virtually since the beginning of the process of deinstitutionalisation, there have been concerns that police officers are becoming de facto providers of mental health. Studies of policing in the 1960s and 1970s (Bittner, 1967, 1970) indicated that the failures of deinstitutionalisation had led to police beat officers becoming increasingly involved in mental health work. In Lipsky's classic *Street level bureaucracy* (1980), police officers described themselves as acting as street-level psychiatrists. Decades later, there is widespread acceptance that people with mental health problems have higher rates of contact with the police than the general population (Teasdale et al, 2014). Radical critics of the current policing role emphasise moves towards militarisation (Harcourt, 2018) and the way that policing is increasingly a response to the problems created by inequality and welfare retrenchment (Vitale, 2017). The role of the police in the mental health field has been shaped by the failure to develop community based mental health services and the expansion of the CJS including imprisonment (Cummins, 2013, 2016).

Police officers report that they find contacts with people with mental health problems a difficult area of work. Police officers regarded this work as time-consuming and often unpredictable. This remains the case despite an increased focus on training for officers in this area (Thomas and Watson, 2017). In countries where the police are routinely armed we know that people with mental health problems are at greater risk of dying in a mental health emergency if the police become involved. This remains the case despite the efforts outlined in this volume to develop new ways of working.

The trends of increased pressure on community mental health teams and greater police involvement in mental health work were apparent in England and Wales in the 1990s. The role of the police was highlighted in several community care inquiries in the 1990s – most notably the Ritchie Inquiry (Ritchie et al, 1994) into the care and treatment of Christopher Clunis. Clunis murdered Jonathan Zito at a tube station in 1992 (Cummins, 2020c). Clunis had contact with the police and a range of other agencies following a series of compulsory admissions under the MHA. The Ritchie Inquiry was critical of the police failure to act on information from members of the public who had contacted them to raise concerns about Clunis' erratic and threatening behaviour. The inquiry concluded that the police had failed to protect the public from potential harm. The Ritchie Inquiry and the media coverage of the case played a key role in the 'community care has failed' narrative (Cummins, 2013). It is noticeable that in the reporting of the inquiry's findings and recommendations there was little real focus on police involvement in the case. This may reflect a less critical attitude to the police in general at that time.

In the current context, there are concerns from the police that they are being increasingly called upon because of the gaps in community mental health services (HMICFRS, 2018). This is a role that police officers often feel ill-equipped to undertake. The police role is thus a combination of preventing crime, detecting and apprehending those who have committed offences and a more general one (Bittner, 1967). This has always been the case since the establishment of the modern police force. However, it is clear that the pressures have increased since the development of deinstitutionalisation and the policies of austerity adopted since 2010 (Cummins, 2018a, 2018b).

The factors that led to the introduction of the policies of deinstitutionalisation and community care were a complex mixture of progressive social values, responses to the abuses of institutionalised psychiatry and fiscal conservatism. In the early years of community care fiscal conservatism was dominant. The progressive vision of a range of well-funded community services, including crisis centres as alternatives to hospital admission, has never materialised. The 1980s and 1990s version of community care could be seen as a polar opposite of the progressive vision. The rise in homelessness and other factors meant that police officers were much more likely to have contact with people in crisis. Contemporary police mental health work is still framed as a response to the failings of deinstitutionalisation and community care narrative. It is important that this discourse does not obscure the other factors at play. For example, welfare retrenchment and the reduction in police numbers has had a hugely significant impact in policing and mental health in the past ten years. In addition, there is a danger that the failing community care narrative might lead to calls for the return of asylums. This might seem fear-mongering. However, one of the lessons of the development of mental health policy since the 1983 MHA is that it is easier to introduce policies that focus on organisational audit and accountability than it is to tackle structural underinvestment in mental health services. In some areas, for example the introduction of CTOs, the result has been the erosion of service-user rights.

The fact that it is so difficult to measure police demand means that the public representation of these issues across the media is even more influential. Leading policing figures such as Sir Ian Blair (2016) and Sir Tom Winsor (2012) have made statements that the demands created by mental health work have meant that the police have been unable to carry out other duties and that this has put the public at risk. In the context of policing and mental health, there is a strong narrative which sees the police being drawn into this realm because of the failings of other agencies – picking up the pieces. This is not to deny the increased demands on the police. It is rather to question whether it is possible to define the police role in such a way so as to exclude all but responses to mental health emergencies. The range of potential situations that police are or might be involved in makes this impossible. In situations such as the potential use of section 136 of the MHA, police officers are the only group with the legal powers to intervene.

Police involvement in mental health work has to be viewed as part of their role in wider community safety and the protection of vulnerable people. Vitale (2017) is extremely critical of what he terms the 'warrior mentality' in modern policing. There are two elements to this. A focus on using force to resolve disputes and the deeply entrenched notion of the 'thin blue line' – the police as the institution that is protecting against societal collapse. Vitale (2017) is writing in a US context. There needs to be some caution in mapping across to the British context. However, one can see that such a mindset will potentially undermine the response to a mental health crisis. The aim should be to de-escalate the situation and recognise that there is not an immediate intervention that will resolve the underlying factors that create a mental health crisis (Carey, 2001; Lurigio and Watson, 2010).

Wood et al's (2011) review of trends in the UK, Canada and the US concluded that the same issues arise across the countries: a combination of reduced psychiatric provision and poorly funded community services has led to increased pressure on police officers who often receive little mental health training. Police officers, particularly in urban areas, deal with incidents that relate in some way or another to mental illness on an almost daily basis. Lord Adebowale (2013) carried out an inquiry into policing and mental health work in the MPS. The inquiry was initially into the death of Sean Rigg in police custody in 2008. Rigg, who had a history of mental illness, died after being restrained by the police. They had been called by support staff at the accommodation where Rigg was living as he had been behaving erratically. Lord Adebowale broadened the scope of his inquiry because of the level of police work that was mental health related. This should be taken to mean that dealing with individuals experiencing mental distress is a key feature of the working week of most police officers. The majority of the recommendations that Lord Adebowale made did not specifically relate to the actions of police officers.

The recommendations of the Adebowale Review

The Adebowale Review laid out a clear blueprint for policing in this field. It is worth looking at the changes the review thought would come about if all its recommendations were implemented:

- that a person in a critical mental state who is found by the police in public and who needs medical care is escorted safely to hospital in an ambulance;
- that the police and NHS staff know what their respective roles are with respect to that individual and that they are treated throughout with respect and without exacerbating their condition;

- that a person in the community who is at high risk of causing serious harm to themselves or another person on account of their mental ill-health and who comes to police notice is referred to partner agencies. If need be, a care plan is put in place for that individual through a multiagency approach in which the police participate
- that the public can be confident that the MPS has a fully professional approach to the protection of life of suicidal individuals, so that any suicidal individual who comes to the notice of the police gets the attention and timely support of a trained professional;
- that the frontline police officer working on the street and in custody has clear and consistent procedures to follow for both planned and unplanned instances involving people with mental health conditions, including access to negotiators where needed and clear referral pathways to other services;
- that a person with a significant mental health problem who is taken into custody has their health care needs dealt with to the same standard as in the NHS; and that during custody, and before their release from custody, they are assessed for suicidality and mental health needs, and provided with referral and support, where appropriate, to liaison and diversion services;
- that a vulnerable person is not released from custody without a positive effort to link them to a carer, relative or professional and place to stay; and that this is recorded in the custody record;
- that the police are trained and provided with accessible guidance and information to assist them to use referral systems efficiently;
- that any person with a significant mental health condition is treated without being stigmatised or discriminated against for their ethnicity or race; and
- that mutually productive relationships, based on respect and good communication exist between all relevant agencies as well as with relatives and carers of people with mental health problems and the police.

It is nearly a decade since the report was published. There has been welcome progress in areas such as the use of police cells, improved training for police officers, new models of interagency working and a recognition of the need to support police officers who are experiencing poor mental health. The challenge is to continue this progress and ensure that this vision can be realised.

Further reading

Adebowale, L. (2013) *Independent commission on mental health and policing report*. Available at: http://mentalhealthpolicing-independent.wazoku.com

Angiolini, E. (2017) *Report of the Independent Review of Deaths and Serious Incidents in Police Custody*. Available at: https://www.gov.uk/government/publications/deaths-and-serious-incidents-in-police-custody

Lane, R. (2019) 'I'm a police officer not a social worker or mental health nurse': online discourses of exclusion and resistance regarding mental health-related police work. *Journal of Community & Applied Social Psychology*, 29(5), 429–442.

McDaniel, J.L. (2019) Reconciling mental health, public policing and police accountability. *The Police Journal*, 92(1), 72–94.

National Police Chiefs Council (2020) *National strategy on policing and mental health*. Available at: https://www.npcc.police.uk/Mental%20Health/Nat%20Strat%20Final%20v2%2026%20Feb%202020.pdf

Williams, E., Norman, J. and Brown, M. (2020) Policing and mental health. in McDaniel, J., Moss, K. and Pease, K. eds., 2020. *Policing and Mental Health: Theory, Policy and Practice*. Abingdon Routledge.

Notes

Chapter 5

[1]   www.nhs.uk/mental-health/conditions/post-traumatic-stress-disorder-ptsd/treatment/

Chapter 6

[1]   www.crisisconcordat.org
[2]   www.crisisconcordat.org
[3]   www.crisisconcordat.org
[4]   www.crisisconcordat.org

References

Aas, K.F. (2014) *Globalization and crime* (2nd edn). London: Sage.

Adams, S. and Riggs, S. (2008) An exploratory study of vicarious trauma among therapist trainees. *Training and Education in Professional Psychology*, 2(1), 26–34.

Adebowale, L. (2013) *Independent commission on mental health and policing report*. Available at: http://mentalhealthpolicing-independent.wazoku.com

Alexander, M. (2012) *The new Jim Crow: mass incarceration in the age of colorblindness*. New York: New Press.

Allen, J., Livingstone, S. and Reiner, R. (1997) The generic context for crime: a content analysis of film synopses, 1945–1991. *Journal of Communication*, 47(4), 89–101.

Angiolini, E. (2017) *Report of the independent review of deaths and serious incidents in police custody*. Available at: https://www.gov.uk/government/publications/deaths-and-serious-incidents-in-police-custody

Association of Chief Police Officers (ACPO) (2012) *The national decision model*. Available at: https://www.app.college.police.uk/app-content/national-decision-model/the-national-decision-model/

Association of Chief Police Officers and the Home Office (2006) *Guidance on the safer detention and handling of persons in police custody*. London: National Centre for Policing Excellence.

Baker, D. (2016) Deaths after police contact in England and Wales: the effects of Article 2 of the European Convention on Human Rights on coronial practice. *International Journal of Law in Context*, 12(2), 162–177.

Baker, D. and Pillinger, C. (2019) 'These people are vulnerable, they aren't criminals': mental health, the use of force and deaths after police contact in England. *The Police Journal*, 93(1), 65–81.

Baker, D. and Pillinger, C. (2020) Deaths after police contact involving people with mental health issues. In J.L.M. McDaniel, K. Moss and K.G. Pease (eds) *Policing and mental health: theory, policy and practice*. Oxon: Routledge, 105–124.

Baldwin, S., Bennell, C., Andersen, J.P., Semple, T. and Jenkins, B. (2019) Stress-activity mapping: physiological responses during general duty police encounters. *Frontiers in Psychology*, 10(2216), 1–17.

Bartkowiak-Théron, I. and Asquith, N.L. (2016) Conceptual divides and practice synergies in law enforcement and public health: some lessons from policing vulnerability in Australia. *Policing & Society*, 27(3), 276–288.

Bartlett, P. and Sandland, R. (2003) *Mental health law policy and practice* (2nd edn). Oxford: Oxford University Press.

Beck, A.T. (1976) *Cognitive therapy and the emotional disorders*. New York: International Universities Press.

Beck, A.T. (1997) The past and future of cognitive therapy. *The Journal of Psychotherapy Practice and Research*, 6(4), 276–284.

Beck, U. (1992) *Risk society: towards a new modernity* (translated from the German by Mark Ritter). London: Sage.

Becker, H.S. (2008) *Outsiders*. London: Simon & Schuster.

Bentall, R. (2004) *Madness explained: psychosis and human nature*. London: Penguin.

Bentall, R. (2016) Mental illness is a result of misery, yet we still stigmatise it. *The Guardian*, 26 February. Available at: https://www.theguardian.com/commentisfree/2016/feb/26/mental-illness-misery-childhood-traumas

Bhui, K., Stansfeld, S., Hull, S., Priebe, S., Mole, F. and Feder, G. (2003) Ethnic variations in pathways to and use of specialist mental health services in the UK: systematic review. *The British Journal of Psychiatry*, 182(2), 105–116.

Bittner, E. (1967) The police on skid-row: a study of peace keeping. American Sociological Review, 32, 699–715.

Bittner, E. (1970) *The functions of the police in modern society*. Chevy Chase: National Institute of Mental Health.

Bittner, E. (1974) 'Florence Nightingale in pursuit of Willie Sutton': A theory of the police. In H. Jacob (ed) *The potential for reform of criminal justice*. Beverly Hills, CA: Sage, pp 217–234.

Bittner, E. (1990) *Aspects of police work*. Boston: Northeastern University Press.

Blair, I. (2016) The police can't continue to pick up the pieces of Britain's mental health cuts. *The Guardian*, 25 October.

Bliss, L. (2020) The movement behind LA's decision to cut its police budget. *Bloomberg*, 4 June. Available at: https://www.bloomberg.com/news/articles/2020-06-04/-people-s-budgets-movement-takes-on-police-reform

Blom-Cooper, L., Hally, H. and Murphy, E. (1995) *The falling shadow*. London: Duckworth.

Boffey, D. (2015) Prescriptions for Ritalin and other ADHD drugs double in a decade. *The Guardian*, 15 August. Available at: https://www.theguardian.com/society/2015/aug/15/ritalin-prescriptions-double-decade-adhd-mental-health

Borschmann, R.D., Gillard, S., Turner, K., Chambers, M. and O'Brien, A. (2010) Section 136 of the Mental Health Act: a new literature review. *Medicine, Science and the Law*, 50(1), 34–39.

Bourdieu, P. (1998) The left hand and the right hand of the state. In P. Bourdieu (ed) *Acts of resistance: against the tyranny of the market*. New York: New Press, 1–10.

Bradley, K. (2009) *The Bradley report: Lord Bradley's review of people with mental health problems or learning disabilities in the criminal justice system*. London: Department of Health.

Braslow, J. (1997) *Mental ills and bodily cures: psychiatric treatment in the first half of the twentieth century*. Oakland: University of California Press.

Braun, V. and Clarke, V. (2006) Using thematic analysis in psychology. *Qualitative Research in Psychology*, 3(2), 77–101.

Brewer, J. (2000) *Ethnography (understanding social research)*. Buckingham: Open University Press.

Brogden, M. and Nijhar, P. (2005) *Community policing: national and international models and approaches*. Cullompton: Willan.

Brough, P., Chataway, S. and Biggs, A. (2016) 'You don't want people knowing you're a copper!' A contemporary assessment of police organisational culture. *International Journal of Police Science & Management*, 18(1), 28–36.

Brown, M. (nd) *MentalHealthCop*. Available at: https://mentalhealthcop. wordpress.com

Browne, D. (2009) Black communities, mental health and the criminal justice system. In J. Reynolds, R. Muston, T. Heller, J. Leech, M. McCormick, J. Wallcraft and M. Walsh (eds) *Mental health still matters*. Basingstoke: Palgrave Macmillan.

Buckley, S.B. (2015) The state, the police and the judiciary in the miners' strike: Observations and discussions, thirty years on. *Capital and Class*, 39(3), pp 419–434.

Buerger, M. (1994) A tale of two targets: limitations of community anticrime actions. *Crime and Delinquency*, 40(3), 411–436.

Burke, M.E. (1994) Homosexuality as deviance: the case of the gay police officer. *British Journal of Criminology*, 34, 192–203.

Butler, A.C., Chapman, J.E., Forman, E.M. and Beck, A.T. (2006) The empirical status of cognitive-behavioral therapy: a review of meta-analyses. *Clinical Psychology Review*, 26(1), 17–31.

Campbell, A.D. (2019) Failure on the front line: how the Americans with Disabilities Act should be interpreted to better protect persons in mental health crisis from fatal police shootings. *Columbia Human Rights Law Review*, 51(1), 313–366.

Campeau, H. (2015) 'Police culture' at work: making sense of police oversight. *British Journal of Criminology*, 55(4), 669–687.

Carey, S.J. (2001) Police officers' knowledge of, and attitudes to mental illness in southwest Scotland. *Scottish Medical Journal*, 46(2), 41–42.

Caveney, N., Scott, P., Williams, S. and Howe-Walsh, L. (2020) Police reform, austerity and 'cop culture': time to change the record? *Policing and society*, 30(10), 1210–1225.

Choongh, S. (1997) *Policing as social discipline*. Oxford: Clarendon Press.

Clarke, J. (2005) Crime and social orders: interrogating the detective story. In J. Muncie and E. McCoughlin (eds) *The problem of crime*. London: Sage, 65–100.

Cockcroft, T. (2014) Police culture and transformational leadership: outlining the contours of a troubled relationship. *Policing: A Journal of Policy and Practice*, 8(1), 5–13.

Coffey, A. and Atkinson, P. (2006) *Making sense of qualitative data.* London: Sage.

Cohen, S. (1972) *Folk devils and moral panics.* London: MacGibbon and Kee.

College of Policing (2015) *Mental vulnerability and illness.* Available at: https://www.app.college.police.uk/app-content/mental-health/mental-vulnerability-and-illness/

College of Policing (nd) National decision model. Available at: https://www.app.college.police.uk/app-content/national-decision-model/the-national-decision-model/

Compton, M., Bahora, M., Watson, A. and Oliva, J. (2008) A comprehensive review of extant research on crisis intervention team (CIT) programs. *Journal of American Academy of Psychiatry and the Law*, 36(1), 47–55.

Corston, J. (chair) (2008) *A report by Baroness Jean Corston of a review of women with particular vulnerabilities in the criminal justice system.* Available at: https://webarchive.nationalarchives.gov.uk/20130206102659/http:/www.justice.gov.uk/publications/docs/corston-report-march-2007.pdf

Costa, T., Passos, F. and Queiros, C. (2019) Suicides of male Portuguese police officers: 10 years of national data. *Crisis*, 40(5), 360–364.

CPS (nd) Special measures. Available at: http://www.cps.gov.uk/legal/s_to_u/special_measures/

Cross, S. (2010) *Mediating madness: mental distress and cultural representation.* Basingstoke: Palgrave Macmillan.

Cummins, I. (2006) A path not taken? Mentally disordered offenders and the criminal justice system. *Journal of Social Welfare and Family Law*, 28(3–4), 267–281.

Cummins, I. (2007) Boats against the current: vulnerable adults in police custody. *Journal of Adult Protection*, 9(1), 15–24.

Cummins, I. (2010) Distant voices, still lives: reflections on the impact of media reporting of the cases of Christopher Clunis and Ben Silcock. *Ethnicity and Inequalities in Health and Social cCare*, 3(4), 18–29.

Cummins, I. (2012) Using Simon's *Governing through crime* to explore the development of mental health policy in England and Wales since 1983. *Journal of Social Welfare and Family Law*, 34(3), 325–337.

Cummins, I. (2013) Policing and mental illness in the era of deinstitutionalisation and mass incarceration: A UK perspective. *International Journal of Criminology and Sociological Theory*, 6(4), 92–104.

Cummins, I. (2016) *Mental health and the criminal justice system: a social work perspective.* Northwich: Critical Publishing.

Cummins, I. (2017) *Critical psychiatry: a biography.* Northwich: Critical Publishing.

Cummins, I. (2018a) *Poverty, inequality and social work: the impact of neoliberalism and austerity politics on welfare provision*. Bristol: Policy Press.

Cummins, I. (2018b) The impact of austerity on mental health service provision: a UK perspective. *International Journal of Environmental Research and Public Health*, 15(6), 1145–1156.

Cummins, I. (2019) *Mental health social work re-imagined*. Bristol: Policy Press.

Cummins, I. (2020a) Policing, vulnerability and mental health. In J.L.M. McDaniel, K. Moss and K.G. Pease (eds) *Policing and mental health: theory, policy and practice*. Oxon: Routledge, 182–200.

Cummins, I. (2020b) Defunding the police: a mental health perspective. *Transforming Society*, 17 August. Available at: http://www.transformingsociety. co.uk/2020/08/17/defunding-the-police-a-mental-health-perspective/

Cummins, I. (2020c) *Mental health services and community care: a critical history*. Bristol: Policy Press.

Cummins, I. (2020d) Mass incarceration and neoliberal penality: a response to Lloyd and Whitehead's *Kicked to the Curb*. *International Journal of Law, Crime and Justice*, 62, 1–9.

Cummins, I. (2021) *Welfare and punishment: from Thatcherism to austerity*. Bristol: Policy Press.

Cummins, I. and Edmondson, D. (2016) Policing and street triage. *Journal of Adult Protection*, 18(1), 40–52.

Cummins, I., Foley, M. and King, M. (2014) '… and after the break': police officers' views of TV crime drama. *Policing: A Journal of Policy and Practice*, 8(2), 205–211.

De Waal, A. (2020) New pathogen, old politics. *Boston Review*, 3 April.

Dehaghani, R. (2016) He's just not that vulnerable: exploring the implementation of the appropriate adult safeguard in police custody. *The Howard Journal of Crime and Justice*, 55(4), 396–413.

Denison, D.R. (1996) What is the difference between culture and organizational climate? A native's point of view on a decade of paradigm wars. *Academy of Management Review*, 21(3), 619–654.

Department of Health (1998) *Modernising mental health services: safe, sound and supportive health services*. London: HMSO.

Department of Health (2002) *Fair access to care services: Guidance on eligibility criteria for adult care services*. LAC (2002)13. London: Department of Health.

Department of Health (2008) *Code of Practice Mental Health Act 1983*, Published pursuant to Section 118 of the Act. London: TSO.

Department of Health and Home Office (2014) *Review of the operation of sections 135 and 136 of the Mental Health Act 1983: review report and recommendations*. London: Department of Health and Home Office. Available at: https://assets.publishing.service.gov.uk/government/uploads/ system/uploads/attachment_data/file/389202/S135_and_S136_of_the_ Mental_Health_Act_-_full_outcome.pdf

Dickinson, T. (2014) *Curing queers*. Manchester: Manchester University Press.

Drucker, E. (2011) *A plague of prisons: the epidemiology of mass incarceration in America*. New York: New Press.

Dunn, J. and Fahy T.A. (1990) Police admissions to a psychiatric hospital: demographic and clinical differences between ethnic groups. *British Journal of Psychiatry*, 156(3), 373–378.

Durcan, G., Saunders, A., Gadsby, B. and Hazard, A. (2014) *The Bradley report five years on: an independent review of progress to date and priorities for further development*. London: Centre for Mental Health. Available at: http://www.centreformentalhealth.org.uk/the-bradley-report-five-years-on

Dyer, R. (2005) *Only entertainment*. Abingdon: Routledge.

Dyer, R. (2013) *The matter of images: essays on representations*. Abingdon: Routledge.

Dyer, W., Steer, M. and Biddle, P. (2015) Mental health street triage. *Policing*, 9(4), 377–387. Available at: https://academic.oup.com/policing/article/9/4/377/2362755/Mental-Health-Street-Triage

Edmiston, D. (2018) *Welfare, inequality and social citizenship: deprivation and affluence in austerity Britain*. Bristol: Policy Press.

Edmondson, D. and Cummins, I. (2014) *Oldham mental health phone triage/RAID pilot project*. Available at: https://www.crisiscareconcordat.org.uk/wp-content/uploads/2015/01/OLDHAMMH_TRIAGE-2.pdf

Elliott-Davies, M. (2019) PFEW demand, capacity and welfare survey 2018: headline Statistics December 2018. *Police Federation*.

Finnegan, A. (2015) The biopsychosocial benefits and shortfalls for armed forces veterans engaged in archaeological activities. *Nurse Education Today*, 47, 15–22.

Fisher, H. (1977) *Report of an inquiry by Sir Henry Fisher into the circumstances leading to the trial of three persons on charges arising out of the death of Maxwell Confait and the fire at 27 Doggett Road, London SE6*. London: HMSO.

Foley, M. and Cummins, I. (2018) Reporting sexual violence on mental health wards. *The Journal of Adult Protection*, 20(2), 93–100.

Foot, J. (2015) *The man who closed the asylums: Franco Basaglia and the revolution in mental health care*. London: Verso.

Foster, J. (2003) Police cultures. In T. Newburn (ed) *The handbook of policing*. Cullompton: Willan, 196–227.

Frederick, T., O'Connor, C. and Koziarski, J. (2018) Police interactions with people perceived to have a mental health problem: a critical review of frames, terminology, and definitions. *Victims & Offenders*, 13(8), 1037–1054.

Freudenberger, H.J. (1974) Staff burn-out. *Journal of Social Issues*, 30(1), 159–165.

Gannoni, A. and Bricknell, S. (2019) *Indigenous deaths in custody: 25 years since the Royal Commission into Aboriginal Deaths in Custody*. Available at: https://www.aic.gov.au/sites/default/files/2020-05/crime-and-justice-research-2019.pdf#page=125

Garland, D. (2004) Beyond the culture of control. *Critical Review of International Social and Political Philosophy*, 7(2), 160–189.

Garrett, P.M. (2007) Making social work more Bourdieusian: why the social professions should critically engage with the work of Pierre Bourdieu. *European Journal of Social Work*, 10(2), 225–243.

Garrett, P.M. (2017) *Welfare words: critical social work and social policy*. London: Sage.

Gershon, R.R., Barocas, B., Canton, A.N., Li, X. and Vlahov, D. (2009) Mental, physical, and behavioral outcomes associated with perceived work stress in police officers. *Criminal Justice and Behavior*, 36(3), 275–289.

Gilroy, P. (1982) The myth of black criminality. In R. Miliband (ed) *The socialist register*. London: Merlin, pp 47–57.

Gilroy, P. (2013) *There ain't no black in the Union Jack*. Abingdon: Routledge.

Goffman, E. (1961) *Asylums: essays on the social situation of mental patients and other inmates*. London: Doubleday.

Goffman, E. (2009) *Stigma: notes on the management of spoiled identity*. New York: Simon & Schuster.

Green, P. (1990) *The enemy without: policing and class consciousness in the miner's strike*. Milton Keynes: Open University Press.

Green, T. and Tong, S. (2019) Policing education: international perspectives. *Policing: A Journal of Policy and Practice*: 1-5.

Grieve, J.D.G. (2015) Historical perspective: British policing and the democratic ideal. In P. Wankhade and D. Weir (eds) *Police services leadership and management perspectives*. London: Springer, 15–26.

Griffin, J.D. and Sun, I.Y. (2018) Do work-family conflict and resiliency mediate police stress and burnout: a study of state police officers. *American Journal of Criminal Justice*, 43(2), 354–370.

Haley, M.J. and Swift, A. (1988) P.A.C.E and the social worker: a step in the right direction? *Journal of Social Welfare and Family Law*, 10(6), 353–373.

Hall, S. (1979) The great moving right show. *Marxism Today*, 23(1), 14–20.

Hall, S. and Wilson, D. (2014) New foundations: pseudo-pacification and special liberty as potential cornerstones for a multi-level theory of homicide and serial murder. *European Journal of Criminology*, 11(5), 635–655.

Hall, S., Critcher, C., Jefferson, T., Clarke, J. and Roberts, B. (2013) *Policing the crisis: mugging, the state and law and order*. Basingstoke: Macmillan.

Hampson, M. (2011) Raising standards in relation to Section 136 of the Mental Health Act 1983. *Advances in Psychiatric Treatment*, 17(5), 365–371.

Harcourt, B.E. (2018) *The counterrevolution: how our government went to war against its own citizens*. New York: Basic Books.

Hearn, J. (2004) From hegemonic masculinity to the hegemony of men. *Feminist Theory*, 5(1), 49–72.

Henry, V.E. (2004) *Death work: police, trauma, and the psychology of survival.* Oxford: Oxford University Press.

Her Majesty's Inspectorate of Constabulary (HMIC) (1999) *Police integrity: securing and maintaining public confidence.* London: Home Office.

Her Majesty's Inspectorate of Constabulary (HMIC) (2013) *A criminal use of police cells? The use of police custody as a place of safety for people with mental health needs.* Available at: http://www.justiceinspectorates.gov.uk/hmic/publication/a-criminal-use-of-police-cells/

Her Majesty's Inspectorate of Constabulary and Fire and Rescue Services (HMICFRS) (2017) *Police custody joint inspection report publications.* Available at: http://www.justiceinspectorates.gov.uk/hmicfrs/?s=&cat = custody-suites-cat&force=&year=&type = publications

HMICFRS (2018) *Policing and mental health: picking up the pieces.* Available at: https://www.justiceinspectorates.gov.uk/hmicfrs/wp-content/uploads/policing-and-mental-health-picking-up-the-pieces.pdf

Hinton, E. (2021) *America on fire: the untold story of police violence and black rebellion.* New York: Liveright Publishing.

HM Inspectorate of Prisons (nd) What we do. Available at: https://www.justiceinspectorates.gov.uk/hmiprisons/about-hmi-prisons/

Holdaway, S. (1983) *Inside the British police.* Oxford: Blackwell.

Holdaway, S. (1986) Police and social work relations: problems and possibilities. *British Journal of Social Work*, 16, 137–160.

Houdmont, J. and Elliott-Davies, M. (2016) *Police Federation of England and Wales: 2016 officer demand, capacity, and welfare survey: initial report – descriptive results.* Available at: www.polfed.org/media/14061/welfare-survey-2016-pfew-descriptive-results-report-v30.pdf

House of Commons Home Affairs Committee (2015) Policing and mental health. Available at: https://publications.parliament.uk/pa/cm201415/cmselect/cmhaff/202/202.pdf

Ignatieff, M. (1985) State, civil society and total institutions. In S. Cohen and A. Scull (eds) *Social control and the state: historical and comparative essays.* Oxford: Blackwell, pp 153–192.

INQUEST (2019) INQUEST responds to deaths in police custody statistics. Available at: https://www.inquest.org.uk/iopc-stats-2019

Intervoice (nd) Available at: http://www.intervoiceonline.org/

IOPC (nd) Death and serious injuries. Available at: https://www.policeconduct.gov.uk/research-and-learning/key-areas-work/death-and-serious-injuries

James, O. (2008) *The selfish capitalist: origins of affluenza.* London: Random House.

Jetelina, K.K., Molsberry, R.J., Gonzalez, J.R., Beauchamp, A.M. and Hall, T. (2020) Prevalence of mental illness and mental health care use among police officers. *JAMA Network Open*, 3(10), e2019658–e2019658.

Jones, S.L. and Mason, T. (2002) Quality of treatment following police detention of mentally disordered offenders. *Journal of Psychiatric and Mental Health Nursing*, 9(1), 73–80.

Kamarudin, K., Zulkafaly, F. and Hassan, N.M. (2018) Role conflict, role ambiguity and job stress among police officers. *International Journal of Academic Research in Business and Social Sciences*, 8(8), 861–873.

Kane, E. (2020) Investment v impact in policing and mental health: what works for police and suspects. In J.L.M. McDaniel, K. Moss and K.G. Pease (eds) *Policing and mental health: theory, policy and practice.* Oxon: Routledge, 83–105.

Karban, K. (2016) Developing a health inequalities approach for mental health social work. *British Journal of Social Work*, 47(3), 885–992.

Kesey, K. (2005) *One flew over the cuckoo's nest.* London: Penguin.

King, M. and Cummins, I. (2014) The violences of men: David Peace's 1974. *Culture Society and Masculinities*, 6(1), 91–108.

Kohan, A. and Mazmanian, D. (2003) Police work, burnout, and pro-organizational behavior: a consideration of daily work experiences. *Criminal Justice and Behavior*, 30(5), 559–583.

Koskela, S.A., Pettitt, B. and Drennan, V.M. (2016) The experiences of people with mental health problems who are victims of crime with the police in England: a qualitative study. *British Journal of Criminology*, 56(5), 1014–1033.

Kringen, A.L. (2014) Scholarship on women and policing: trends and policy implications. *Feminist Criminology*, 9(4), 267–381.

Lamb, H.R., Weinberger, L.E. and DeCuir, W.J. (2002) The police and mental health. *Psychiatric Services*, 46(12), 1267–1271.

Lamb, V. and Tarpey, E. (2019) 'It's not getting them the support they need': exploratory research of police officers' experiences of community mental health. *The Police Journal: Theory, Practice and Principles*, 92(4), 277–295.

Lane, R. (2019) 'I'm police officer not a social worker or mental health nurse': online discourses of exclusion and resistance regarding mental health-related police work. *Journal of Community & Applied Social Psychology*, 29(5), 429–442.

Latham, A. (1997) The Cinderella section: room for improvement in the documentation and implementation of section 136 of the Mental Health Act 1983. *Journal of Clinical Forensic Medicine*, 4(4), 173–175.

Laufs, J., Bowers, K., Birks, D. and Johnson, S.D. (2020) Understanding the concept of 'demand' in policing: a scoping review and resulting implications for demand management. *Policing and Society*, 31(8), 1–24.

Lea, J. (1987) Left realism: a defence. *Contemporary Crises*, 11(4), 21–32.

Lea, J. (1992) The analysis of crime. In J. Young and R. Matthews (eds) *Rethinking criminology: the realist debate*. London: Sage, pp 69–94.

Lea, J. (2002) *Crime and modernity*. London: Sage.

Lea, J. (2016) Left realism: a radical criminology for the current crisis. *International Journal for Crime, Justice and Social Democracy*, 5(3), 53–65.

Leishman, F. and Mason, P. (2003) *Policing and the media: facts, fictions and factions*. Cullompton: Willan.

Lipsky, M. (1980) *Street-level bureaucracy: dilemmas of the individual in public services*. New York: Russell Sage Foundation.

Loader, I. (2013) Why do the police matter? Beyond the myth of crime-fighting. In J. Brown (ed) *The future of policing*. London: Routledge, 40–51.

Loader, I. (2016) In search of civic policing: recasting the 'Peelian' principles. *Criminal Law and Philosophy*, 10(3), 427–440.

Loader, I. and Mulcahy, A. (2003) *Policing and the condition of England: memory, politics and culture*. Oxford: Oxford University Press.

Local Authority Circular LAC (2002) *Fair access to care services: guidance on eligibility criteria for adult social care*, 13. London: Department of Health.

Loftus, B. (2009) *Police culture in a changing world*. Oxford: Oxford University Press.

Loftus, B. (2010) Police occupational culture: classic themes altered times. *Policing and Society*, 20(1), 1–20.

Lombroso, C. (2012) *Crime, its causes and remedies*. London: Forgotten Books.

Lurigio, A. and Watson, A.C. (2010) The police and people with mental illness: new approaches to a longstanding problem. *Journal of Police Crisis Negotiations*, 10(1–2), 3–14.

Macpherson, S.W. (1999) *The Stephen Lawrence inquiry: report of an inquiry by Sir William Macpherson of Cluny*. London: HMSO.

Manthorpe, J., Rapaport, J., Harris, J. and Samsi, K. (2009) Realising the safeguarding potential of the Mental Capacity Act 2005: early reports from adult safeguarding staff. *Journal of Adult Protection*, 11, 13–24.

Marmot, M. (2010) *Fair society, healthy lives: the Marmot review*. London: Department of Health. Available at: www.parliament.uk/documents/fair- society- healthy- lives- full- report.pdf

Marsden, M., Nigam, J., Lemetyinen, H. and Edge, D. (2020) Investigating police officers' perceptions of their role in pathways to mental healthcare. *Health & Social Care in the Community*, 28(3), 913–921.

Martin, J. (2002) *Organizational culture: mapping the terrain*. Thousand Oaks: Sage.

Maslach, C. (1976) Burnout. *Human Behavior*, 5, 16–22.

Maslach, C. (1982). *Burnout: the cost of caring*. New York: Prentice Hall.

Matthews, R. (2010) The construction of 'so what?' criminology: realist analysis, *Crime, Law and Social Change*, 54(2), 125–140.

McCann, I.L. and Pearlman, L. (1990) Vicarious traumatisation: a framework for understanding the psychological effects of working with victims. *Journal of Traumatic Stress*, 3(1), 131–149.

McCarty, W.P. and Skogan, W.G. (2012) Job-related burnout among civilian and sworn police personnel. *Police Quarterly*, 16(1), 66–84.

McCarty, W.P., Zhao, J. and Garland, B.E. (2007) Occupational stress and burnout between male and female police officers: are there any gender differences? *Policing: An International Journal of Police Strategies & Management*, 30(4), 672–691.

McDaniel, J.L. (2019) Reconciling mental health, public policing and police accountability. *The Police Journal*, 92(1), 72–94.

McLaughlin, E. (2007) *The new policing*. London: Sage.

McLean, N. and Marshall, L.A. (2010) A front line police perspective of mental health issues and services. *Criminal Behaviour and Mental Health*, 20(1), 62–71.

Medford, S., Gudjonsson, G.H. and Pearse, J. (2003) The efficacy of the appropriate adult safeguard during police interviewing. *Legal and Criminological Psychology*, 8(2), 253–266.

Meikle, J. (2016) Antidepressant prescriptions in England double in a decade. *The Guardian*, 5 July. Available at: https://www.theguardian.com/society/2016/jul/05/antidepressant-prescriptions-in-england-double-in-a-decade

Millie, A. and Bullock, K. (2013) Policing in a time of contraction and constraint: re-imagining the role and function of contemporary policing. *Criminology and Criminal Justice*, 13(2), 133–142.

MIND (2015) *At risk yet dismissed*. Available at: https://www.mind.org.uk/media-a/4121/at-risk-yet-dismissed-report.pdf

MIND (2020) *The mental health emergency*. Available at: https://www.mind.org.uk/media-a/5929/the-mental-health-emergency_a4_final.pdf

Moncrieff, J. (2004) Is psychiatry for sale: an examination of the influence of the pharmaceutical industry on academic and practical psychiatry. Available at: http://www.critpsynet.freeuk.com/pharmaceuticalindustry.htm

Moon, G. (2000) Risk and protection: the discourse of confinement in contemporary mental health policy. *Health & Place*, 6(3), 239–250.

Morabito, M. (2007) Horizons of context: understanding the police decision to arrest people with mental illness. *Psychiatric Services*, 58(12), 1582–1587.

Morgan, M. and Patterson, C. (2017) 'It's mental health, not mental police': a human rights approach to mental health triage and Section 136 of the Mental Health Act 1983. *Policing*, 13(2), 123–133.

Murphy, R. (director) (2010) *Nordic noir*. BBC TV.

NAAN (2015) *There to help*. National Appropriate Adult Network. Available at: www.appropriateadult.org.uk/index.php/policy/policy-publications/there-to-help.

NAAN (2019) *There to help 2*. National Appropriate Adult Network. Available at: www.appropriateadult.org.uk/index.php/policy/policy-publications/there-to-help.

National Police Chiefs Council (2020) *National strategy on policing and mental health*. National Police Chiefs Council. Available at: https://www.npcc.police.uk/Mental%20Health/Nat%20Strat%20Final%20v2%2026%20Feb%202020.pdf

Neely, P. and Cleveland, C.S. (2011) The impact of job-related stressors on incidents of excessive force by police officers. *American Journal of Health Sciences*, 3(1), 63–74.

Newburn, T. and Hayman, S. (2002) *Policing, surveillance and social control: CCTV and police monitoring of suspects*. Cullompton: Willan.

Neyroud, P. and Weisburd, D. (2014) Transforming the police through science: the challenge of ownership. *Policing*, 8(4), 287–293.

NHS Confederation (2015) *Mental health and policing improving crisis care*. NHS Confederation. Available at: http://www.nhsconfed.org/~/media/Confederation/Files/public%20access/Briefing%20279%20Mental%20health%20and%20policing%20final%2026%20Jan.pdf

O'Neill, M. and McCarthy, D. (2014) (Re)negotiating police culture through partnership working: trust, compromise and the 'new' pragmatism. *Criminology and Criminal Justice*, 1(2), 143–159.

Papazoglou, K., Koskelainen, M., Tuttle, B.M. and Pitel, M. (2017) Examining the role of police compassion fatigue and negative personality traits in impeding the promotion of police compassion satisfaction: a brief report. *Journal of Law Enforcement*, 6(1), 1–14.

Papazoglou, K., Blumberg, D.M., Chiongbian, V.B., Tuttle, B.M., Kamkar, K., Chopko, B., Milliard, B., Aukhojee, P. and Koskelainen, M. (2020) The role of moral injury in PTSD among law enforcement officers: a brief report. *Frontiers in Psychology*, 11(310), 1–6.

Park, A., Booth, A., Parker, A.J., Scantlebury, A., Wright, K. and Webber, M. (2019) Models of mental health triage for individuals coming to the attention of the police who may be experiencing mental health crisis: a scoping review. *Policing: A Journal of Policy and Practice*, 15(2), 859–895.

Parr, H. and Stevenson, O. (2013) *Missing people, missing voices: stories of missing experience*. Available at https://eprints.gla.ac.uk/84048/1/84048.pdf

Parsons, A.E. (2019) *From asylum to prison: deinstitutionalization and the rise of mass incarceration after 1945*. Chapel Hill: UNC Press Books.

Paton, D., Violanti, J., Johnston, P., Clarke, J., Burjke, K. and Keenan, D. (2008) Stress shield: a model of police resiliency. In L. Territo and J.D. Sewell (eds) *Stress management in law enforcement* (3rd edn). Durham, NC: Carolina Academic Press, 501–522.

Payne-James, J.J. (2016) Risk factors for death or harm to health for detainees in short-term police custody. In J. Gall and J. Payne (eds) *Current Practice in Forensic Medicine*, Chichester: John Wiley and Sons, pp 79–206.

Perez, L.M., Jones, J., Englert, D.R. and Sachau, D. (2010) Secondary traumatic stress JOand burnout among law enforcement investigators exposed to disturbing media images. *Journal of Police and Criminal Psychology*, 25(2), 113–124.

Philo, C. (1987) 'Fit localities for an asylum': the historical geography of the nineteenth century 'mad-business' in England as viewed through the pages of the *Asylum Journal. Journal of Historical Geography*, 13(4), 398–415.

Pickett, K. and Wilkinson, R. (2009) *The spirit level: why equality is better for everyone*. London: Penguin.

Pierpoint, H. (2000) How appropriate are volunteers as appropriate adults for young suspects? The appropriate adult's system and human rights. *The Journal of Social Welfare & Family Law*, 22(4), 383–400.

Plath, S. (2005) *The bell jar*. London: Faber & Faber.

Powell, E. (1961) *Integration*. Available at: http://enochpowell.info/wp-content/uploads/Speeches/1957-1961.pdf

Punch, M. (1979) *The secret social service*. In S. Holdaway (ed) *The British police*. London: Hodder & Stoughton, pp 17–34.

Puntis, S., Perfect, D., Kirubarajan, A., Bolton, S., Davies, F., Hayes, A., Harriess, E. and Molodynski, A. (2018) A systematic review of co-responder models of police mental health 'street' triage. *BMC Psychiatry*, 18(1), 1–11.

Purnell, D. (2021) *Becoming abolitionists: police, protest, and the pursuit of freedom*. London: Verso Books.

Queirós, C., Fernando, P., Bártolo, A., Marques, A., Da Silva, C. and Pereira, A. (2020) Burnout and stress measurement in police officers: literature review and a study with the operational police stress questionnaire. *Frontiers in Psychology* 11, 587.

Reiner, R. (1985) A watershed in policing. *The Political Quarterly, 56*(2), 122–131.

Reiner, R. (1992a) Policing a postmodern society. *The Modern Law Review*, 55(6), 761–781.

Reiner, R. (1992b) *The politics of the police*, 2nd edn. London: Harvester Wheatsheaf.

Reiner, R. (2010) *The politics of the police*. Oxford: Oxford University Press.

Reuss-Ianni, E. and Ianni, F.A.J. (1999) Street cops and management cops: the two cultures of policing. In M. Punch (ed) *Control in the police organisation*. Cambridge, MA: MIT Press.

Reveruzzi, B. and Pilling, S. (2016) *Street triage: report on the evaluation of nine pilot schemes in England*. Available at: https://s16878.pcdn.co/wp-content/uploads/2016/09/Street-Triage-Evaluation-Final-Report.pdf

Riley, G., Freeman, E., Laidlaw, J. and Pugh, D. (2011) A frightening experience: detainees' and carers' experiences of being detained under Section 136 of the Mental Health Act. *Medicine, Science and the Law*, 51(3), 164–169.

Ritchie, J., Dick, D. and Lingham, R. (1994) *Report of the inquiry into the care and treatment of Christopher Clunis*. London: HMSO.

Roach, J., Cartwright, A. and Sharratt, K. (2017) Dealing with the unthinkable: a study of the cognitive and emotional stress of adult and child homicide investigations on police investigators. *Journal of Police and Criminal Psychology*, 32(3), 251–262.

Roach, J., Sharratt, K., Cartwright, A. and Skou Roer, T. (2018) Cognitive and emotional stressors of child homicide investigations on UK and Danish police investigators. *Homicide Studies*, 22(3), 296–320.

Rodgers, M., Thomas, E., Dalton, J.E., Harden, M. and Eastwood, A.J. (2019) Police related triage interventions for mental health related incidents: a rapid evidence synthesis. *Health Services and Delivery Research*, 7(20).

Rogers, A. and Faulkner, A. (1987) *A place of safety*. London: MIND Publications.

Rogers, C. and Wintle, E. (2020) Accessing justice for mental health sufferers? A comparison of UK and Australian developments. In J.L.M. McDaniel, K. Moss and K.G. Pease (eds) *Policing and mental health: theory, policy and practice*. Oxon: Routledge, pp 38–59.

Rosa, J., Passos, F. and Queirós, C. (2015) Um estudo exploratório sobre burnout e indicadores psicopatológicos em polícias. *International Journal of Working Conditions*, 10, 101–119.

Russell, H. (2017) *The use of force and article 2 of the ECHR in light of European conflicts*. Portland: Hart Publishing.

Sackmann, S. (1991) *Cultural knowledge in organizations*. Newbury Park, CA: Sage.

Sainsbury Centre for Mental Health (2008), Police and mental health. Available at: www.centreformentalhealth.org.uk/pdfs/briefing36_police_and_mental_health.pdf

Sands, N., Elsom, S., Gerdtz, M., Henderson, K., Keppich-Arnold, S., Droste, N., Prematunga, R.K. and Wereta, Z.W. (2013) Identifying the core competencies of mental health telephone triage. *Journal of Clinical Nursing*, 22(21–22), 3203–3216.

Scarman, J., Lord (1981) *The Brixton disorders, 10–12th April (1981)*. London: HMSO.

Schaufeli, W.B. (2017) Burnout: a short socio-cultural history. In S. Neckel, A. Schaffner and G. Wagner (eds) *Burnout, fatigue, exhaustion*. Cham: Palgrave Macmillan, 105–127.

Schrag, P. (2004) *Paradise lost: California's experience, America's future: updated with a new preface*. Oakland: University of California Press.

Scull, A. (1987) Book review: Joan Busfield, *Managing madness: changing ideas and practice*, London, Hutchinson, 1986, 8vo, pp 406, £25.00. *Medical History*, 31(4), 484–485.

Scull, A. (2011) *Madness: A very short introduction*. Oxford Oxford University Press.

Scull, A. (2014) *Madness in civilization: a cultural history of insanity from the Bible to Freud, from the madhouse to modern medicine*. Princeton: Princeton University Press.

Shapiro, G.K., Cusi, A., Kirst, M., O'Campo, P., Nakhost, A. and Stergiopoulos, V. (2015) Co-responding police-mental health programs: a review. *Administration and Policy in Mental Health and Mental Health Services Research*, 42(5), 606–620.

Sherman, L.W. (2020) Evidence-based policing and fatal police shootings: promise, problems, and prospects. *The Annals of the American Academy of Political and Social Science*, 687(1), 8–26.

Sigurdsson, J. and Dhani, A. (2010) *Police service strength England and Wales*, 31 March. Available at: https://assets.publishing.service.gov.uk/government/uploads/system/uploads/attachment_data/file/115745/hosb1410.pdf

Simon, J. (2007) *Governing through crime: how the war on crime transformed American democracy and created a culture of fear*. Oxford: Oxford University Press.

Singleton, N., Meltzer, H. and Gatward, R. (1998) *Psychiatric morbidity among prisoners in England and Wales*. London: Office for National Statistics.

Skinner, B.F. (2002) *Beyond freedom and dignity*. London: Hackett Publishing.

Skinner, B.F. (2012) The experimental analysis of behavior. *American Scientist*, 100(1), 54–60.

Skinns, L. (2011) *Police custody: governance, legitimacy and reform in the criminal justice process*. Abingdon: Routledge.

Skogan, W. (2008) Why reforms fail. *Policing and Society*, 18(1), 23–34.

Slasberg, C. and Beresford, P. (2014) Government guidance for the Care Act: undermining ambitions for change? *Disability & Society*, 29(10), 1677–1682.

Social Care Institute for Excellence (nd) Available at: www.scie.org.uk

Sondhi, A. and Williams, E. (2019) Police and health operational staff perspectives on managing detainees held under Section 136 of the Mental Health Act: a qualitative study in London. *Journal of Community Safety and Well-Being*, 4(4), 88–93.

Sondhi, A., Luger, L., Toleikyte, L. and Williams, E. (2018) Patient perspectives of being detained under section 136 of the Mental Health Act: findings from a qualitative study in London. *Medicine, Science and the Law*, 58(3), 159–167.

Steel, J., Thornicroft, G., Birmingham, L., Brooker, C., Mills, A., Harty, M. and Shaw, J. (2007) Prison mental health in-reach services. *British Journal of Psychiatry*, 190, 373–374.

Szmukler, G. (2018) *Men in white coats: treatment under coercion*. Oxford: Oxford University Press.

Teasdale, B., Daigle, L.E. and Ballard, E. (2014) Trajectories of recurring victimization among people with major mental disorders. *Journal of Interpersonal Violence*, 29(6), 987–1005.

Teplin, L.A. (1984) Criminalizing mental disorder: the comparative arrest rate of the mentally ill. *American Psychologist*, 39(7), 794–803.

Thomas, S. (2020) Critical essay: fatal encounters involving people experiencing mental illness. *Salus Journal*, 8(2), 100–116.

Thomas, S. and Watson, A. (2017) A focus for mental health training for police. *Journal of Criminological Research, Policy and Practice*, 3(2), 93–104.

Trades Union Congress (2018) *Breaking point: the crisis in mental health funding*. Trades Union Congress. Available at: https://www.tuc.org.uk/research-analysis/reports/breaking-point-crisis-mental-health-funding

Truss, L. (2020) The new fight for fairness. Speech. Available at: https://youtu.be/V0Vhrn82QtE

Tuckey, M.R. and Scott, J.E. (2013) Group critical incident stress debriefing with emergency services personnel: a randomized controlled trial. *Anxiety, Stress & Coping*, 27(1), 38–54.

Tyler, I. (2020) *Stigma: the machinery of inequality*. London: Zed Books.

Varese, F., Smeets, F., Drukker, M., Lieverse, R., Lataster, T., Viechtbauer, W., Read, J., Van Os, J. and Bentall, R.P. (2012) Childhood adversities increase the risk of psychosis: a meta-analysis of patient-control, prospective- and cross-sectional cohort studies. *Schizophrenia Bulletin*, 38(4), 661–671.

Violanti, J.M. (1996) *Police suicide: epidemic in blue*. Springfield: Charles C. Thomas.

Violanti, J.M. (2010) Police suicide: a national comparison with fire-fighter and military personnel. *International Journal of Police Strategies & Management*, 33(2), 270–286.

Violanti, J.M., Vena, J.E. and Petralia, S. (1998) Mortality of a police cohort: 1950–1990. *American Journal of Industrial Medicine*, 33(4), 366–373.

Violanti, J.M., Owens, S.L., McCanlies, E., Fekedulegn, D. and Andrew, M.E. (2019) Law enforcement suicide: a review. *Policing: An International Journal of Police Strategies & Management*, 42(2), 141–164.

Vitale, A.S. (2017) *The end of policing*. London: Verso.

Wacquant, L. (1998) Pierre Bourdieu. In R. Stone (ed) *Key sociological thinkers*. London: Palgrave, 215–229.

Wacquant, L. (2002) From slavery to mass incarceration. *New Left Review*, 13(1), 41–60.

Wacquant, L. (ed) (2005) *Pierre Bourdieu and democratic politics: the mystery of ministry*. Cambridge: Polity.

Waddington, P. (1999) Police (canteen) sub-culture: an appreciation. *British Journal of Criminology*, 39(2), 287–309.

Walley, P. and Adams, M.M. (2019) *An evaluation of demand management practices in UK police forces*. Available at: www.open.ac.uk

Watson, A.C., Morabito, M.S., Draine, J. and Ottati, V. (2008) Improving police response to persons with mental illness: a multi-level conceptualization of CIT. *International Journal of Law and Psychiatry*, 31(4), 359–368.

Webb, S.A. (2006) *Social work in a risk society: social and political perspectives*. Basingstoke: Macmillan.

Weinfass, I. (2015) Deeply concerning deterioration in rank and file morale. *Police Oracle*, 14 July. Available at: http://www.policeoracle.com/news/HR_personnel_and_staff_development/2015/Jul/13/-deeply-concerning–deterioration-of-rank-and-file-morale_88903.html

Weisburd, D. and Neyroud, P. (2011) New perspectives in policing. Cambridge, MA: Harvard University Press.

Wessley, S. (2018) Independent review of the Mental Health Act. London: Department of Health.

Westmarland, L. and Rowe, M. (2016) Police ethics and integrity: can a new code overturn the blue code? *Policing and Society*, 28(7), 854–870.

Williams, E., Norman, J. and Brown, M. (2020) Policing and mental health. In J. McDaniel, K. Moss and K. Pease (eds) *Policing and mental health: theory, policy and practice*. Abingdon: Routledge, pp 201–220.

Winsor, T. (2012) *Report into police pay and conditions*. London: Home Office.

Wolff, N. (2005) Community reintegration of prisoners with mental illness: a social investment perspective. *International Journal of Law and Psychiatry*, 28(1), 43–58.

Wood, J., Swanson, J., Burris, J.D. and Gilbert, A. (2011) *Police interventions with persons affected by mental illnesses: a critical review of global thinking*. New York: Rutgers University, Center for Behavioral Health Services and Criminal Justice Research.

Wood, J., Watson, A.C. and Fulambarker, A.J. (2017) The 'gray zone' of police work during mental health encounters: findings from an observational study in Chicago. *Police Quarterly*, 20(1), 81–105.

World Health Organization (2008) Trencin statement on prisons and mental health. Available at: https://apps.who.int/iris/bitstream/handle/10665/108575/E91402.pdf

Young, J. (2002) From inclusive to exclusive society: Nightmares in the European dream. In *The new European criminology*. Abingdon: Routledge, pp 82–110.

Legal cases

DPP v Blake (1989) W.L.R 432 89 Cr App L.R 179.

R v Cox (1991) Crim LR 276.

R v Morse (1991) Crim LR 195.

Index

Page numbers in **bold** type refer to tables.